21st Century Economics

Bruno S. Frey • Christoph A. Schaltegger
Editors

21st Century Economics

Economic Ideas You Should Read and Remember

 Springer

Editors
Bruno S. Frey
University of Basel
CREMA
Zurich, Switzerland

Christoph A. Schaltegger
University of Lucerne
Department of Economics
Lucerne, Switzerland

ISBN 978-3-030-17739-3   ISBN 978-3-030-17740-9   (eBook)
https://doi.org/10.1007/978-3-030-17740-9

This Springer imprint is published by the registered company Springer Nature Switzerland AG.
The registered company address is: Gewerbestrasse 11, 6330 Cham, Switzerland

Introduction

Modern economics is a vivid, dynamic and relevant social science—this is the firm conviction of the two editors.

But what is the content of modern economics? What should one read and remember?

In order to find out, we asked a number of young and old, beginning and accomplished, professional economists. We did not in any way interfere in what the contributions should contain; the contributors were completely free to choose any text they wanted.

There were only three requirements. The text recommended to be read and remembered:

- Must be publicly available. It can be an article, a book or any other type of publication.
- Must have been published since the year 2000. While we fully acknowledge the major impact exerted on economics by scholars like Adam Smith, Karl Marx, Joseph Schumpeter or John Maynard Keynes, we wanted to know what modern texts are recommended.
- The contribution must not exceed 3500 characters and must recommend only one text.

The result is this book containing recommendations to read and remember by 61 contributors. They come from many different countries and make a large number of different proposals. This illustrates that economics in the twenty-first century is indeed a vivid and dynamic discipline. It is up to the reader whether, and to what extent, the proposed texts are relevant for the real world.

The editors are convinced that this is the case.

University of Basel   Bruno S. Frey
Basel, Switzerland

CREMA – Center for Research in Economics
Management and the Arts
Zurich, Switzerland

University of Lucerne   Christoph A. Schaltegger
Lucerne, Switzerland

Contents

About the Editors

Bruno S. Frey is Permanent Visiting Professor at the University of Basel. He was Professor of Economics at the University of Zurich from 1977 to 2012; Distinguished Professor of Behavioural Science at the Business School of Warwick University, UK, from 2010 to 2013; and Senior Professor of Economics at Zeppelin University Friedrichshafen, Germany, from 2013 to 2015.

Frey is Research Director of CREMA—Center for Research in Economics, Management and the Arts, Switzerland, and Co-Founder of CREW—Center for Research in Economics and Well-being at the University of Basel. He was Managing Editor from 1969 to 2015 and is now Honorary Editor of *Kyklos*. Bruno Frey seeks to extend economics beyond the standard neo-classics by including insights from other disciplines, including political science, psychology and sociology.

Christoph A. Schaltegger has been Professor of Political Economics at the University of Lucerne since 2010. Since 2016, he has acted as the Dean of the Faculty of Economics and Management. He also teaches public finance at the University of St. Gallen, where he serves as a director of the Institute of Public Finance and Fiscal Law (IFF). In spring 2009, he was Visiting Scholar at the Queensland University of Technology in Brisbane (Australia).

The editors want to thank Evelyn Holderegger for the excellent work and great help in editing this volume. They are also grateful to Gabriela Rychener for her support and especially to Dr Simon Milligan for his careful proofreading.

Christine Benesch Recommends "Mostly Harmless Econometrics: An Empiricist's Companion" by Joshua D. Angrist and Jörn-Steffen Pischke

Christine Benesch

>> *Angrist and Pischke are not the first or only ones to present econometric methods for causal inference and emphasize the importance of a credible research design. However, by writing an accessible, concise, and even fun-to-read textbook, they have made the concepts and methods palatable to a large audience.*

It might be a bit surprising to find an econometric textbook in a collection of "economic ideas you should remember." *Mostly Harmless Econometrics: An Empiricist's Companion* by Joshua Angrist and Jörn-Steffen Pischke, however, is far more than a textbook. Not only does it differ from traditional econometric textbooks because of its catchy title and refreshing language, but its focus on identification of causal effects and quasi-experimental analysis has also—for better or worse—influenced an entire generation of (micro)economists in their approach to empirical research.

The book starts with the question whether hospitals make people healthier in order to illustrate the selection problem empirical researchers are plagued

C. Benesch (✉)

University of St. Gallen, St. Gallen, Switzerland

e-mail: christine.benesch@unisg.ch

© Springer Nature Switzerland AG 2019

B. S. Frey, C. A. Schaltegger (eds.), *21st Century Economics*,

https://doi.org/10.1007/978-3-030-17740-9_1

with when analyzing observational data. While people who have recently been to the hospital might be less healthy than those who have not, going to the hospital does not necessarily make people sicker. People who go to the hospital are of poorer health to begin with. A simple comparison of people who have and have not been to the hospital will thus lead to faulty conclusions. Random assignment, though it could solve the selection problem, is often not feasible. Angrist and Pischke therefore discuss alternative methods for causal inference—such as regression with controls, instrumental variable approach, difference-in-difference analysis, and regression discontinuity design. Since all the methods are well illustrated with examples of empirical studies, the intuition behind the empirical approaches is always comprehensible, even if the reader decides to skip the formal parts of the chapters.

The presented methods all emphasize research design as the key element for credible empirical studies. Angrist and Pischke are convinced that such a focus on better and more transparent research design has led to a "credibility revolution in empirical economics" and a subsequent increase in policy relevance and scientific impact of empirical research. Nonetheless, the allegedly narrow focus of the design-based approach has sparked a heated debate in economics. One concern is that the concentration on identification of causal effects and quasi-experimental methods might create incentives for researchers to ignore many policy-relevant questions—especially if alternative approaches such as structural modeling or time series analysis are discredited as less plausible (to which potential referees might agree). Hence, researchers might decide that an analysis is simply not worthwhile in cases where the institutional setup impedes the analysis of a natural experiment. Still, the design-based approach can be applied to a wide array of questions and "good research designs complement good questions," as Angrist and Pischke write in an article in the *Journal of Economic Perspectives* in 2010.

Angrist and Pischke are not the first or only ones to present econometric methods for causal inference and emphasize the importance of a credible research design. However, by writing an accessible, concise, and even fun-to-read textbook, they have made the concepts and methods palatable to a large audience. Thus, anyone interested in credible empirical research should read *Mostly Harmless Econometrics* and remember its ideas.

Literature

Angrist, J. D., & Pischke, J.-S. (2009). *Mostly harmless econometrics: An empiricist's companion*. Princeton: Princeton University Press.

Matthias Benz Recommends "The Political Economy of Government Responsiveness: Theory and Evidence from India" by Tim Besley and Robin Burgess

Matthias Benz

>> *As ad revenues shrink dramatically mainly for newspapers, independent high-quality journalism is under pressure. The question of how it can survive in the digital age is of great importance for well-functioning democracies, as the work of Besley and Burgess has shown.*

"There are no famines in democracies," Nobel-Prize winning economist Amartya Sen famously argued. It is less well known that he also stressed the role of a free press. In his view, politicians have to take the well-being of the citizens more into account if they run the risk of being voted out or if their actions are monitored by free media.

In an article published in 2002, Tim Besley and Robin Burgess presented the first thorough test of these ideas. They showed that regional governments in India provided more emergency assistance to people affected by natural disasters if newspaper circulation was higher. This was convincing evidence that the "fourth estate" indeed affects politics. The paper helped to launch a

M. Benz (✉)
University of Vienna, Vienna, Austria

Neue Zürcher Zeitung, Zurich, Switzerland
e-mail: matthias.benz@nzz.ch

© Springer Nature Switzerland AG 2019
B. S. Frey, C. A. Schaltegger (eds.), *21st Century Economics*,
https://doi.org/10.1007/978-3-030-17740-9_2

new field of media economics, which has become a rising star in the discipline and has greatly improved our understanding of how the media impact politics and the economy.

Economists had long been dealing with the question of what makes good politics. But the paper by Besley and Burgess was the first in-depth study of how the media can mitigate the so-called principal–agent problem (meaning that governments often do not act in the interest of their citizens). Their theoretical model leads to the central hypothesis that politicians pay more attention to citizens' interests if the prevalence of media is larger. The reason for this is that their actions become more visible.

Besley and Burgess tested their model empirically. The context is still highly relevant: How do politicians react to natural disasters such as droughts or floods? Recently, a great famine was imminent in, say, East Africa. The authors showed that it is the media—in this case the prevalence of local language regional newspapers—that make politicians more responsive to citizens' needs. Subsequent papers in the field have corroborated that public authorities in the West react to media coverage in similar ways. The importance of media reporting has also been shown for economic contexts, such as for the quality of corporate governance in firms.

The emerging field of media economics has provided evidence that the media serve as a "fourth estate." But Besley and co-authors have also looked at the conditions under which the media can perform this function more or less successfully. Their theories suggest that the media can better control politics when (a) there is more competition between media outlets, (b) the media are not state-owned, and (c) the media can rely on larger and broader revenues from commercial sources such as ads and subscriptions.

These insights are relevant for the current digital revolution in the media sector. An important question is how the "watchdog" function is changed by the advent of social media such as Facebook or Twitter. On the one hand, economic reasoning suggests that the role of the "fourth estate" is strengthened, because the market for information becomes bigger, better accessible, and more competitive. For instance, social media have fostered the Arab Spring and civic protests in China. On the other hand, the ascent of social media is eroding the power of the "fourth estate," mainly because internet companies like Facebook or Google take a large part of the advertisement market. As ad revenues shrink dramatically mainly for newspapers, independent high-quality journalism is under pressure. The question of how it can survive in the digital age is of great importance for well-functioning democracies, as the work of Besley and Burgess has shown.

Literature

Besley, T., & Burgess, R. (2002). The political economy of government responsiveness: Theory and evidence from India. *Quarterly Journal of Economics, 117*(4), 1415–1451.

Aleksander Berentsen Recommends "Bitcoin: A Peer-to-Peer Electronic Cash System" by Satoshi Nakamoto

Aleksander Berentsen

The most important contribution in economics in the twenty-first century is the paper *Bitcoin: A Peer-to-Peer Electronic Cash System*. It was published via a mailing list for cryptography in 2008 under the pseudonym Satoshi Nakamoto. The basic idea of the paper was to create "A purely peer-to-peer version of electronic cash [that] would allow online payments to be sent directly from one party to another without going through a financial institution."

The Bitcoin developers have linked several technological components together to create a virtual asset that is substantially different from any other asset. For the first time, ownership of virtual property is possible without the need for a central authority—a development with the potential to fundamentally change the current financial system and many areas in business and government.

Our current financial infrastructure relies on centrally managed accounting systems. Centralization creates several problems. First, all transactions are recorded in one place leading to lack of privacy. Second, a central point of attack (internal as well as external) for manipulation attempts is created. Third, the entity endowed with such a monopoly right can become systemically important. Fourth, such a position could be abused (rent-seeking). Fifth, the central authority has the possibility of excluding individuals and/or confiscating their assets.

A. Berentsen (✉)
Center for Innovative Finance, University of Basel, Basel, Switzerland
e-mail: aleksander.berentsen@unibas.ch

© Springer Nature Switzerland AG 2019
B. S. Frey, C. A. Schaltegger (eds.), *21st Century Economics*,
https://doi.org/10.1007/978-3-030-17740-9_3

Bitcoin made it possible to represent virtual assets in a decentrally managed accounting system. Each participant is able to keep a copy of the ledger and verify each transaction independently instead of blindly trusting a centralized entity. A clever consensus protocol ensures that at any point of time, all participants agree on the distribution of ownership for all Bitcoin units. The consensus building in a decentralized network, where network participants don't know and therefore cannot trust each other, is Bitcoin's true innovation.

A decentralized accounting system avoids the problems of centralization mentioned above and provides additional benefits. First, the decentralized nature of record keeping combined with sophisticated cryptography makes it difficult if not impossible to manipulate the database ex post. Second, Bitcoin is very resilient. The Bitcoin network has had no down time since its implementation in 2009. Third, the user can own his data and can be his own bank.

As with any fundamental innovation, the true potential of decentralized accounting systems will become apparent only many years, or possibly decades, after it is widely adopted. As of now, the most apparent application is the provision of a censorship-resistant asset. It is likely that cryptoassets will emerge as their own asset class and develop into an interesting investment and diversification instrument. Bitcoin itself could over time assume a role similar of that of gold. Furthermore, any real asset can be represented as a virtual asset (tokenization) and traded worldwide without intermediaries on decentralized networks. Other applications are smart contracts and distributed autonomous organizations. Finally, because it is very difficult to change records retroactively, decentralized accounting systems can be used to serve as proof that a specific data file existed in a particular form at a specific point in time.

We have just seen the beginning. We are currently witnessing a Cambrian explosion of ideas, projects, and startups, and I'm excited to observe live in the coming years where this experiment leads us.

Literature

Nakamoto, S. (2008). *Bitcoin: A peer-to-peer electronic cash system.* https://bitcoin.org/bitcoin.pdf

Thomas Bernauer Recommends "Tracking the Ecological Overshoot of the Human Economy" by Mathis Wackernagel, Niels B. Schulz, Diana Deumling, Alejandro Callejas Linares, Martin Jenkins, Valerie Kapos, Chad Monfreda, Jonathan Loh et al.

Thomas Bernauer

>> *Pioneering ideas from ecological economics and life-cycle assessment (LCA), spearheaded by Rees, Wackernagel, Wiedmann, Peters, and others, are shedding new light on how international trade has led to environmental burden-shifting in the global economy.*

The Environmental Kuznets Curve (EKC), one of the most important models in environmental economics, holds that societies with very low levels of economic output impose only a small burden on their natural environment. With industrialization the ecological impact increases, reaches a peak, and then starts to decline as the so-called economic scale effect is offset by two other factors: (1) the composition of the economy changes, with less polluting activity, such as services and light manufacturing, increasing; and (2) the

T. Bernauer (✉)
Institute of Science, Technology and Policy (ISTP), ETH Zurich,
Zurich, Switzerland
e-mail: thbe0520@ethz.ch

© Springer Nature Switzerland AG 2019
B. S. Frey, C. A. Schaltegger (eds.), *21st Century Economics*,
https://doi.org/10.1007/978-3-030-17740-9_4

financial and technical ability of societies to become more resource efficient per unit of economic output grows, and so does the willingness of people to incur opportunity costs from environmental protection (post-material preferences). These dynamics result, hypothetically, in an inverted U-shaped relationship between income levels and environmental impacts of economic activity. The EKC model has motivated countless empirical studies. Despite mixed results and criticism, it has helped us identify why particular environmental problems are easier to solve than others as economies grow.

A glaring gap in the EKC model is, nonetheless, that economies may not only become greener endogenously. They may also achieve greater domestic environmental quality by offloading environmental impacts of consumption beyond their borders. Pioneering ideas coming out of ecological economics and life-cycle assessment (LCA) since the mid- to late 1990s, spearheaded by Rees, Wackernagel, Wiedmann, Peters, and others, are shedding new light on such environmental burden-shifting processes in the global economy. They point to the fact that international trade is associated with a geographic dissociation of production and consumption. Using LCA and large amounts of disaggregated trade data has then allowed researchers, motivated by this idea, to systematically distinguish environmental impacts of consumption from those of production. It turns out that most rich countries have become greener domestically only in part because of the mechanisms of the EKC but to a large degree by shifting environmental impacts of their consumption onto other countries or the global atmosphere and oceans. For instance, if the average person on our planet burdened the environment at the same level as the average resident of Switzerland, a very rich, green, and open economy, we would need three Earths.

While many economic ideas are fascinating primarily to academic economists, the idea of distinguishing production- from consumption-related environmental impacts is a very powerful and policy-relevant idea. In Switzerland, for instance, it has already led to a national vote on including a "one Earth" ecological target, to be achieved by 2050, into the constitution. 36% voted yes: not enough to enact the proposal, but enough to keep the idea alive, which is evident from the many green economy initiatives at national and international levels.

Over the coming years, the idea of distinguishing consumption- from production-related ecological impacts could change our conventional territorial notions of what international environmental externalities are. This, in turn, would have big implications for how international trade liberalization and environmental agreements are designed and responsibilities among nations are assigned.

Literature

Wackernagel, M., Schulz, N. B., Deumling, D., Linares, A. C., Jenkins, M., Kapos, V., Monfreda, C., Loh, J., et al. (2002). Tracking the ecological overshoot of the human economy. *Proceedings of the National Academy of Sciences of the United States of America, 99*(14), 9266–9271.

Peter Bernholz Recommends "Redesigning Democracy: More Ideas for Better Rules" by Hans Gersbach

Peter Bernholz

» *Hans Gersbach has been working since the 1990s to design democratic systems better able to prevent the unfortunate developments. His present book describes a newly invented political mechanism adequate to fulfill just this task.*

In his speech in the House of Commons on Nov. 11, 1947, Winston Churchill pronounced the famous dictum: "Democracy is the worst form of government, except for all those other forms that have been tried from time to time."

Churchill was and is still right. Fundamental problems remain even within the best existing democracies. The Hobbesian problem remains that the monopoly of government power, necessary to maintain the rule of law, can still lead to a deterioration of a democratic system guaranteeing freedom of citizens and an adequate provision of public goods. Such a development can presently again be observed in countries like Venezuela and Turkey. And this is in spite of the initially existing separation of power into the legislative, executive, and judiciary branches of government, which has been an accomplishment of the last 300 years.

P. Bernholz (✉)

Prof. em., Faculty of Business and Economics, WWZ, University of Basel, Basel, Switzerland

e-mail: peter.bernholz@unibas.ch

© Springer Nature Switzerland AG 2019

B. S. Frey, C. A. Schaltegger (eds.), *21st Century Economics*,

https://doi.org/10.1007/978-3-030-17740-9_5

Hans Gersbach has been working since the 1990s to design democratic systems better able to prevent the unfortunate developments. His present book describes a newly invented political mechanism adequate to fulfill just this task. It comprises two different parts. The first part (Contractual Democracy) proves how, with the introduction of contracts proposed by competing political candidates, the results of their policies after their election can be improved for the citizens. Here the problem is studied that inferior short-term projects ripening in the first election period may be selected over superior long-term projects because the latter can only come to fruition in the second election period. The second part of the book (Rules for Decision-Making and Agenda-Setting) demonstrates how better political rules and agendas for offering a divisible public good can lead to optimal outcomes, in contrast to the present situation.

Part I discusses an important problem in using contracts with political candidates to improve the democratic system. Because there are millions of voters, it is impossible for them to conclude contracts offered by the candidates for political office. Gersbach circumvents this difficulty by introducing an independent authority, which also has the task of assessing the performance of the politicians in fulfilling the contract. The candidate who succeeds in the first election receives a reward or a penalty according to how he implements the contract he has concluded. The question, however, what might be the interests of the authority that is partner to the contract is not discussed.

In Part 2 of the book, the provision of a variable level of a public good financed by taxes is discussed within the framework of a democratic constitution when aggregate shocks are absent. It is shown that an efficient provision occurs if four rules are met.

An important insight is the following: In the case of aggregate shocks to benefits and costs, the efficiency of democratic constitutions can be preserved if the supermajority rules of the first case are replaced by tax-sensitive rules, where the required majority is a strictly monotonically increasing function of aggregate tax revenues.

Another insight is that it is always possible to find a democratic constitution that leads to a Pareto-improvement compared to the status quo.

One can only hope that existing political systems will be prepared to introduce in time the proposed reforms.

Literature

Gersbach, H. (2017). *Redesigning democracy: More ideas for better rules.* New York: Springer.

Norbert Berthold Recommends "The Son Also Rises: Surnames and the History of Social Mobility" by Gregory Clark

Norbert Berthold

》 *Recent studies on intergenerational mobility usually measure economic success based on income and wealth. Gregory Clark, however, pursued a broader approach, which also includes education, occupation, and life expectancy as indicators of the social position.*

The growing level of income inequality over the past decades has intensified the interest in social mobility. The prospect of social advancement appeases the "relative" losers. Therefore, social mobility may be considered the glue that holds unequal societies together, both intra- and intergenerationally. However, solid empirical studies on intergenerational income mobility are scarce. Such studies require complete dataset covering multiple generations. Microlevel income data, however, is usually only available for a few generations, which is why most of the empirical analyses take into account the mobility level across only two or three generations. Consequently, these studies do not provide a reliable indication of the long-term development of intergenerational mobility. Such an assessment requires data from multiple generations, which may

N. Berthold (✉)

Institute of Economics, University of Würzburg, Würzburg, Germany

e-mail: norbert.berthold@uni-wuerzburg.de

© Springer Nature Switzerland AG 2019

B. S. Frey, C. A. Schaltegger (eds.), *21st Century Economics*,

https://doi.org/10.1007/978-3-030-17740-9_6

15

be at hand only in the distant future. But Gregory Clark, a Scottish economic historian at the University of California in Davis, did not want to wait that long. He examined how the social status of families developed over many centuries. Since upper-class families often have rare and offbeat names, he had the ingenious idea of using surnames as indicators. He was able to show that in professions with a high social prestige, such as doctors, lawyers, professors, and parliamentarians, the upper class was disproportionately represented many generations ago. In fact, this has not changed until today and implies that social mobility may be lower than often assumed.

Recent studies on intergenerational mobility usually measure economic success based on income and wealth. Gregory Clark, however, pursued a broader approach, which also includes education, occupation, and life expectancy as indicators of the social position. Based on this approach, he analyzed different countries whose institutional change has been very different over the past centuries, including the United Kingdom, the United States, Sweden, Japan, China, India, South Korea, and Chile. Despite considerable data issues, Gregory Clark was able to acquire information on the social status of individuals that goes back many centuries. Perhaps the most prominent and innovative way to collect data was his usage of surnames of students that were enrolled in the Universities of Cambridge and Oxford. Studying at these universities was clearly a privilege in the past, and one that was reserved for the elite. A particular benefit of this strategy is that data on students' names is fully preserved back to the Middle Ages. The results of his analysis are spectacular: In each of the investigated cases, long-run *im*mobility is quite high. In contrast to more recent studies that find an intragenerational elasticity of 15–45%, Clark's analysis implies figures of 70% and higher.

This result is a severe blow for the "American Dream." Clark's findings imply that individual social success is "hereditary" and is hardly influenced by the environment: "Nature predominates over nurture." Apparently, the position on the social ladder is determined by the coincidence of birth. In a performance-oriented society, however, the iron law of the "regression to the mean" makes social up- and downturns inevitable. Yet marriage behavior has slowed down this dynamic during the past centuries, as marriage within the same social class keeps mobility rates low.

Literature

Clark, G. (2014). *The son also rises: Surnames and the history of social mobility.* Princeton: Princeton University Press.

Urs Birchler Recommends "Why Every Economist Should Learn Some Auction Theory" by Paul Klemperer

Urs Birchler

A few years ago, I attended a conference with some of the best researchers from finance and micro. The greatest impression, though, was made by a practitioner from a consulting firm, sharing his experience with auctioning off of failed financial firms. After a brilliant presentation, commenting on his last slide, he wondered why successful bidders had to pay the second highest bid only, rather than their own, highest, bid.

The embarrassed finance people stared into their desks. What had happened? This brilliant speaker had just displayed his ignorance of one of the most fundamental, and famous, results of auction theory known as the revenue equivalence theorem (RET). William Vickrey, in 1961, had shown that (under some assumptions) all auction formats lead to the same expected revenue. In a first-price auction (as proposed by our speaker), bidders bid more cautiously than in a second-price auction (as used in his examples), such that both yield the same expected revenue to the seller.

Had the speaker only known Paul Klemperer's paper "Why Every Economist Should Learn Some Auction Theory"! Klemperer claims that auction theory is not a remote province of economic thinking, but at the core of economics—just recall the good old Walrasian auctioneer. And often, auctions come in disguise, as in court litigations, architectural competitions, or even marital arguments.

U. Birchler (✉)
Prof. em., University of Zurich, Zurich, Switzerland
e-mail: urs.birchler@bf.uzh.ch

Klemperer casts an auction-theoretical light on a number of economic topics: financial crashes, queues, rationing, wars of attrition, valuing new customers, e-commerce, and, as mentioned, litigation systems. Some of the insights follow directly from the RET: Making litigation cheaper does not reduce litigation expense in equilibrium. Offering chairs or soda to people queuing will lead to longer queues, not to less disutility.

One example Klemperer could not have known at the time he wrote his article is Bitcoin "mining," a typical case of an all-pay auction (like litigation, queuing, and architectural contests). To the degree that bidders "pay" with time, effort, or inconvenience, which are lost to the "seller" (the judge, the movie theater, the builder), all-pay auctions are inefficient (revenue equivalence here meaning cost equivalence).

Klemperer's paper has a companion, written in the same year and published in the *Journal of Economic Perspectives* in 2002, titled "What really matters in auction design." When the RET does not apply (due to some assumptions being violated), small mistakes make big losses. Due to poor design, auctions of spectrum licenses for "third-generation" mobile phones in 2000 yielded only 20 Euros per head of population in Switzerland (compared to 600 Euros in Germany).

Not only economists benefit from reading Klemperer's work. A title "Why *everybody* should learn some auction theory" would have been quite appropriate, as Klemperer could have shown with two further examples: corporate drinking and marital arguments. If nobody wants to be the one who had the second-last, rather than the last drink, regret will follow. And if none of two partners wants to "lose" an argument by having the second-last word both will lose more than the argument.

Literature

Klemperer, P. (2000). *Why every economist should learn some auction theory* (CEPR Discussion Papers 2572).

Luigino Bruni Recommends "The Idea of Justice" by Amartya Sen

Luigino Bruni

> ❱❱ *The Idea of Justice is (so far) Sen's last published theoretical treatise. Among the several topics of the book, I think that the criticism of the idea of happiness deserves serious consideration by any scholar of subjective well-being and, in general, social scientists.*

Amartya Sen is most probably the most well-known and relevant philosopher–economist of the present generation. In the last 40 years, he has given contributions to ethics and philosophy of economics that have become milestones of contemporary debate.

Well-being, capabilities, freedom, agency, fairness and justice, and human development are topics that today are intrinsically linked to Sen's works.

The Idea of Justice is (so far) Sen's last published theoretical treatise. Among the several topics of the book, I think that the criticism of the idea of happiness deserves serious consideration by any scholar of subjective well-being and, in general, social scientists. In his vision and critique of happiness, most of Sen's ideas of economics and philosophy are synthesized. Sen has often radically

L. Bruni (✉)
University LUMSA, Rome, Italy
e-mail: l.bruni@lumsa.it

© Springer Nature Switzerland AG 2019
B. S. Frey, C. A. Schaltegger (eds.), *21st Century Economics*,
https://doi.org/10.1007/978-3-030-17740-9_8

criticized Bentham's utilitarianism and that vision of happiness—the maximization of social and individual pleasures—as it is incompatible with his general theory of capabilities and freedom. In this book, however, Sen also criticizes the much broader idea of happiness that we find in Aristotle (*eudaimonia*) and in J.S. Mill, which is at the basis of many contemporary scholars of happiness. Sen tells us that even when the limits of the concept of happiness are broadened to include the idea of fulfillment or human flourishing, which for the Aristotelian tradition is the supreme and ultimate good, happiness is not the only variable that counts in life, nor the most important one. If, by reinterpreting Aristotle, happiness were to become all that has value in a person's life, then happiness would become a useless concept for social analysis, since knowing that all good and true things trace back to happiness leaves us without any criterion for specific choices, which frequently feature a conflict between several good situations. For Sen, then, one should keep happiness within the boundaries of common sense, including utilitarian happiness, considering it as but *one dimension* of life that in certain instances can give way to others.

I have worked for several years around the idea of Aristotelian happiness, showing that many of the criticisms of the studies on happiness are actually applicable to Bentham's, rather than Aristotle's, view.

I now agree with Sen. As an example, consider a person (a woman, as Sen often does) who for religious, cultural, or ideological reasons is convinced that being subject to her husband is part of her vocation, and she is content and happy in that condition. If she begins a path of awareness and liberation and so increases her capabilities, certainly in the early stages, and perhaps even in later ones, her subjective happiness will decrease, but her freedom will increase. Can we then say that the woman is happier while possibly suffering spiritually and perhaps physically? I do not know; we can, however, say with certainty that she is freer and thus prefers to trigger the process of her becoming aware, even though we know that there will be a cost in terms of subjective happiness. We could certainly include freedom in her happiness, in an Aristotelian sense; but, again, in so doing the concept of happiness would become so broad as to be useless. Happiness is important but is too little for a good life: "One does not have to be a Gandhi (or a Martin Luther King, or a Nelson Mandela, or Aung San Suu Kyi) to understand that one's objectives and priorities could stretch well beyond the narrow limits of one's own personal well-being" (p. 290).

Literature

Sen, A. (2009). *The idea of justice* (467 pp). Cambridge: The Belknap Press of Harvard University Press.

Monika Bütler Recommends "The Economic Importance of Financial Literacy: Theory and Evidence" by Annamaria Lusardi and Olivia S. Mitchell

Monika Bütler

>> *Given the importance of financial decisions on individuals' well-being, it is surprising how little we knew about the level of financial literacy. Until the ground-breaking work of Annamaria Lusardi and Olivia S. Mitchell, the profession did not even have a meaningful measure of financial literacy.*

Interest compounding, accounting for inflation, and diversification of risks—economists know the importance of such knowledge for sound financial decisions. Noneconomists should know as well. Financial skills are essential for many decisions: to finance a home, the children's education, or providing for rainy days. The higher the amount of money invested or spent, the greater the potential mistakes, and thus the more important financial knowledge is. Mistakes can have severe, often irreversible consequences. Too many individuals end up in debt or do not manage to save enough for retirement.

Given the importance of financial decisions on individuals' well-being, it is surprising how little we knew about the level of financial literacy, as we call these skills today, in the population. Surprisingly too, these valuable skills are

M. Bütler (✉)
SEW-HSG, University of St. Gallen, St. Gallen, Switzerland
e-mail: monika.buetler@unisg.ch

© Springer Nature Switzerland AG 2019
B. S. Frey, C. A. Schaltegger (eds.), *21st Century Economics*,
https://doi.org/10.1007/978-3-030-17740-9_9

hardly taught at school. Until very recently, the profession did not even have a meaningful measure of financial literacy.

That is where Annamaria Lusardi and Olivia Mitchell stepped in. Motivated by huge differences in retirement wealth among otherwise similar elderly households, the two researchers thought about meaningful and simple ways to measure financial knowledge. They convinced the well-known US Health and Retirement Study to add three questions to its 2004 survey.

Today known as the big 3, the questions read as follows:

1. "Suppose you had $100 in a savings account and the interest rate was 2% per year. After 5 years, how much do you think you would have in the account if you left the money to grow?" (A) More than $102, (B) Exactly $102, (C) Less than $102
2. "Imagine that the interest rate on your savings account was 1% per year and inflation was 2% per year. After 1 year, with the money in this account, would you be able to buy…" (A) More than today, (B) Exactly the same as today, (C) Less than today
3. "Do you think the following statement is true or false? Buying a single company stock usually provides a safer return than a stock mutual fund." (A) True, (B) False

For each of the three questions, the respondents can also choose (D) Don't know or (E) Refuse to answer. These additional options turned out to be incredibly useful for the interpretation of the findings.

If you think the questions are trivial, think twice (or better still, read the paper): overall, only about 50% of the respondents get all the answers right, more in some countries, less in others. Schooling obviously helps, but even among college graduates, approximately 30% get at least one answer wrong. Middle-aged individuals score better than both younger and older ones.

Women always fare worse. However, rather than resort to guessing, they also tick "do not know" or "refuse" more often. Women are less confident, but they also have fewer opportunities to invest. Indeed, follow-up research by the same authors demonstrated that financial knowledge is endogenous.

What started as a small but ingenious exercise paved the way to financial literacy as a new research area and numerous policy initiatives worldwide. Research on financial literacy uncovers heterogeneity, allowing easier targeting of educational interventions. Since its onset, the initiative to increase financial literacy has gained so much momentum that many consider the concept primarily as a policy tool. But behind a seemingly simple idea lies true academic spirit and hard work. It is a bit like in figure skating: The more elegant an exercise appears, the more effort is behind it.

[Correct answers: (1 = A), (2 = C), (3 = B)]

Literature

Lusardi, A., & Mitchell, O. S. (2014). The economic importance of financial literacy: Theory and evidence. *Journal of Economic Literature, 52*(1), 5–44.

Peter Cauwels Recommends "Critical Transitions in Nature and Society" by Marten Scheffer

Peter Cauwels

>> *Financial, economic, and social systems are complex, and we need to understand their moving parts if we want to implement effective policies. The book by Scheffer demonstrates that to study these, one should follow a scientific methodology that is balanced between inductive and deductive reasoning.*

Your favorite band just finished a much-awaited live show. They saved their epic hit single for last, and the crowd bursts in ecstatic applause. At first, the handclapping is quirky; everyone is in their own flow. It sounds like raindrops ticking on a metal roof. Then, something happens. Randomness dissolves and the audience organizes a regular beat. There is no maestro conducting the crowd. This collective behavior emanates from the system itself.

Now, picture a spectator who is a keen observer and a diligent number cruncher. Fascinated by this display of synchronicity, he decides to study the phenomenon. After going through numerous time series of random applause, he manages to construct a fancy statistical model. However, his onerous number crunching conjectures that the synchronicity could not possibly have hap-

P. Cauwels (✉)
Quaerens CommV, Bruges, Belgium

© Springer Nature Switzerland AG 2019
B. S. Frey, C. A. Schaltegger (eds.), *21st Century Economics*,
https://doi.org/10.1007/978-3-030-17740-9_10

pened, with any statistical significance, in the period since the inception of the universe.

Simplified like this, it is obvious that his model is fatally flawed. As the system shifts from random to synchronized, its identity changes. A model designed on a meticulous observation of Dr. Jekyll will never be suitable to predict the demeanor of Mr. Hyde.

As evident as this example may be, very similar methodological misconceptions are deeply ingrained in the current generally accepted framework of financial theory. Markets are considered to be efficient, asset prices follow a random walk, and bubbles and crashes, those events of synchronicity, always catch financial pundits by surprise.

Schizophrenic shifts, as seen in applause, can be observed in many dynamical systems in physics, chemistry, biology, ecology, the climate, human beings, and societies. Even though the agents in these different systems are incomparable on a micro scale, the aggregated behavior on the macro level shows surprising similarities, such as the occurrence of alternative stable states, feedback mechanisms, cycles, hysteresis, emerging patterns, self-organization, finite time singularities with regime shifts, and critical transitions.

In his book, *Critical Transitions in Nature and Society*, Martin Scheffer, a Dutch professor at Wageningen University, presents a comprehensive methodology to study such systems. This is based on the construction of toy models that consist of the essential structural components and all the possible dynamic interactions between them. As Scheffer demonstrates, this may sometimes lead to quite counterintuitive insights. An illustrative example is the fact that terrestrial vegetation can affect oceanic circulation patterns. Needless to say, an insufficient understanding of all the moving parts in a system, be it physical or social, may lead to fallacies and the implementation of inappropriate policies that lead to unintended consequences.

Financial, economic, and social systems are complex, and we need to understand their moving parts if we want to implement effective policies. The book by Scheffer demonstrates that to study these, one should follow a scientific methodology that is balanced between inductive and deductive reasoning. In times when big data and fancy analysis tools prevail, the methodological balance is shifting ever more toward the inductive. However, if we want to obtain a deeper understanding of our complex world, and design policies to enhance its resilience, we need to bring the balance back. For that, not only is data analysis needed and the construction of solid statistical tools but also creativity, imagination, and the ability to find patterns and hidden connections.

Literature

Scheffer, M. (2009). *Critical transitions in nature and society*. Princeton: Princeton University Press.

Sir Paul Collier Recommends "Identity Economics: How Our Identities Shape Our Work, Wages, and Well-Being" by George A. Akerlof and Rachel E. Kranton

Paul Collier

❯❯ *Identity Economics has opened a new field and a professional association, ERINN (Economic Research on Identity, Norms and Narratives). Identity Economics has broadened its concepts from groups and norms, adding narratives that circulate in social networks, and the quest for esteem.*

Identity Economics is an accessible account of rigorous and highly original work by outstanding economists. Akerlof has a Nobel Prize; Kranton is the Editor of *The Economic Journal*. Standard economics has embarrassingly little to say about the crises engulfing Western societies, failing to predict the financial crisis and silent on the mounting social crisis. *Identity Economics* provides a manageable approach to addressing such issues: it restores economics as a *social* science while retaining a framework in which economic tools are applied.

The key idea is to recognize that people live in societies and so understand themselves and others as socially distinct, belonging to different groups. Thinking of oneself as a particular type of person, which is what AK mean by 'identity', comes with consequences: for a person to maintain her own

P. Collier (✉)
Blavatnik School of Government, Oxford University, Oxford, UK
e-mail: Paul.collier@bsg.ox.ac.uk

© Springer Nature Switzerland AG 2019
B. S. Frey, C. A. Schaltegger (eds.), *21st Century Economics*,
https://doi.org/10.1007/978-3-030-17740-9_11

self-image and to be valued as a member of the group, she has to behave in a certain way. Namely, a person has to comply with the social norms for behaviour. Different groups can have different criteria for judging behaviour, and people will need to learn them. Succinctly expressed, people want self-esteem and *esteem* of other group members and hence need to comply with group *norms*. By putting this desire to follow the norms in the utility function, alongside consumption, the conventional economic assumption that rational behaviour implies utility maximization has a radical new implication. Rationally, a person may choose to have lower consumption in order to establish or maintain the desire to belong: we trade off consumption against esteem.

The concept of rationality is agnostic about the content of preferences, but in practice, economists have conventionally shrivelled preferences to consumption and leisure, as in a typical textbook. *Some* assumptions about preferences are essential: allowing them to be exogenous, unspecified and idiosyncratic would remove all predictive power. Much of the book shows that in a range of important situations, by adding belonging and its pressures to conform to group norms, alongside consumption, we improve the predictive power of our utility-maximizing models, an example being behaviour in gangs.

So, is this a better approximation to the human condition? Are humans hardwired to belong as well as to consume? Recent discoveries in socio-biology and neuroscience have vindicated AK. We now know that during human evolution, habitats became more demanding, requiring enlargement of group size from 40 to 150 (the 'Dunbar Constant' of *homo sapiens*). Brain size tripled in order to cope with the demands of increased sociality. We also know that the infant brain evolves into the adult mind through group interaction. *We are social animals* not merely atomistic individuals. Any manageable assumption about preferences is a simplification; modelling is a matter of judgment. For some purposes a conventional utility function is good enough; but economics has come to grief by applying it in contexts where the addition of identity is essential.

Identity Economics has opened a new field and a professional association, ERINN (*Economic Research on Identity, Norms and Narratives*). If people belong to groups that have norms, the process by which they are acquired needs to be specified. Identity Economics has broadened its concepts from *groups* and *norms*, adding *narratives* that circulate in *social networks*, and the quest for *esteem*.

Literature

Akerlof, G. A., & Kranton, R. E. (2010). *Identity economics. How our identities shape our work, wages, and well-being.* Princeton: Princeton University Press.

Reto Cueni Recommends "Too Much Finance?" by Jean-Louis Arcand, Enrico Berkes, and Ugo Panizza

Reto Cueni

» *Yes, say Jean-Louis Arcand, Enrico Berkes, and Ugo Panizza, there can be "too much finance." In their IMF working paper from 2012, they show in a sound empirical analysis that countries with small and intermediate financial sectors benefit from a growing financial sector, that is, more lending to the private sector. However, after a certain threshold, a larger financial sector starts to exert negative effects on economic growth. This is an important message that is often forgotten until today.*

Can there be too much finance in a country? No, of course not, many would argue. Why should firms having easy access to banks, which finance their new projects or the renovation of their infrastructure, be a problem? Until now,

The opinions expressed are those of the author and do not necessarily reflect the views of Vontobel Asset Management.

R. Cueni (✉)
Vontobel Asset Management, Zurich, Switzerland
e-mail: reto.cueni@vontobel.com

more bank lending in a country is usually seen as a positive impulse inducing more economic growth.

Yes, say Jean-Louis Arcand, Enrico Berkes, and Ugo Panizza, there can be "too much finance." In their IMF working paper from 2012, they show in a sound empirical analysis that countries with small and intermediate financial sectors benefit from a growing financial sector, that is, more lending to the private sector. However, in contrast to earlier literature, they show that this relationship is nonlinear and that there is a threshold after which lending becomes negative. They locate this threshold at around 100% credit to the private sector as a percentage of a country's gross domestic product (GDP). After this point, a growing financial sector is on average detrimental to economic growth. Of course, the optimal size of "finance" depends on many difficult-to-capture variables, such as the institutional framework in a country (e.g., to which extent interest on credit can be deducted from taxes). However, the authors run estimations controlling for some institutional differences and still find a significant threshold for "too much finance."

Why is this paper important to read and remember? The finding might sound like common sense, and several eminent scholars such as Hyman Minsky, Charles Kindleberger, or James Tobin, among others, made a similar point long time ago. Yet, the idea that "more finance is always better for economic growth" is until this day difficult to refute. Many central bankers as well as investment professionals and politicians talk, write, and act as if more lending were always better for the economy.

The paper's findings, and the findings in later studies confirming them, help adjust our view on how lending actually supports growth. Of course, banks and other financial intermediaries are important as they transform short-dated and often small deposits into long-dated and often larger credits by allocating monetary resources to, hopefully, socially useful and profit-generating investments. Banks absorb and share or adopt risks for a potential failure of repayment of borrowers. There is a vast amount of real-life examples and literature confirming that a liquid and accessible banking system is very important for economic growth. However, it should be obvious that a credit boom can also become a drag on economic growth, in particular when it is accompanied by decreasing lending standards and a fast-growing financial industry, which is usually the case. Related research has demonstrated that, paradoxically, industries which are more dependent on financing, such as R&D-intensive companies, can suffer even more from a quickly growing financial industry as it absorbs skilled labor. Similarly, financial intermediaries compete with nonfinancial intermediaries for financial resources and create a shortage of credit for the latter.

We should acknowledge that too much credit growth can become negative for economic growth. We need more research and insights into identifying exactly when credit growth becomes a bane for a specific country. This is particularly important today given that global credit to the private sector reached 130% of world GDP in 2016 and, according to data from the World Bank, is still growing.

Literature

Arcand, J. L., Berkes, E., & Panizza, U. (2015). Too much finance? *Journal of Economic Growth, 20*(2), 105–148. (This study was first published as an IMF Working Paper in 2012 (WP/12/161)).

Jakob de Haan Recommends "Why Nations Fail: The Origins of Power, Prosperity, and Poverty" by Daron Acemoglu and James Robinson

Jakob de Haan

Economists have for some time recognized that institutions play an important role in explaining differences in the wealth and poverty of nations. But whereas most previous research focuses either on economic or political institutions, this book offers an excellent framework explaining how both economic and political institutions drive long-run economic development. Whereas economic institutions shape incentives to become educated, to save and invest, and to innovate and adopt new technologies, political institutions determine what economic institutions a country has.

Institutions can be either inclusive, expanding the political and economic opportunities to the broad cross-section of society, or extractive, allowing the elites to extract rents and resources from the rest of the society. Inclusive economic institutions feature secure private property, an unbiased system of law and a provision of public services that provides a level playing field in which people can exchange and contract. Inclusive political institutions have two features: they are (1) pluralistic and (2) centralistic and powerful. The first part of the definition captures what is usually called democracy. But this is not enough: the state needs a sufficiently high level of political centralization, as society otherwise sooner or later descends into chaos.

J. de Haan (✉)
De Nederlandsche Bank, Amsterdam, The Netherlands

University of Groningen, Groningen, The Netherlands
e-mail: jakob.de.haan@rug.nl

© Springer Nature Switzerland AG 2019
B. S. Frey, C. A. Schaltegger (eds.), *21st Century Economics*,
https://doi.org/10.1007/978-3-030-17740-9_13

Extractive economic institutions depend on extractive political institutions for their survival. Extractive economic institutions, in turn, enrich the elites, and their economic wealth and power and help consolidate their political dominance. Unfortunately, societies do not necessarily adopt institutions that are best for economic growth or the welfare of its citizens, simply because other institutions may better foster the interests of those who control politics and political institutions. Notably, fear of "creative destruction" is often at the root of the opposition to inclusive economic and political institutions.

Still, institutions do change. So what drives institutional change? A key role is played by "critical junctures": "During critical junctures, a major event or confluence of factors disrupts the existing balance of political or economic power in a nation" (p. 106). One such critical junction that affected institutional change is European colonialism. Based on their level of urbanization, several countries that were relatively rich in 1500 are now poor. This reversal in fortune reflects changes in the institutions resulting from European colonialism. And this reversal in fortune is, so the argument goes, mostly a late eighteenth- and early nineteenth-century phenomenon and is closely related to industrialization. It is not related to the extraction of resources from the former colonies, or to the direct effect of the diseases Europeans brought to the New World, as in that case the reversal should have taken place shortly after colonization. But the type of colonization matters: Europeans were more likely to introduce institutions encouraging investment ("institutions of private property") in regions with low population density and low urbanization, while they introduced extractive, investment-depressing institutions in richer regions. And such extractive institutions turned out to be inappropriate with the arrival of new technologies during the Industrial Revolution.

Literature

Acemoglu, D., & Robinson, J. A. (2012). *Why nations fail. The origins of power, prosperity and poverty*. London: Profile Books.

Reiner Eichenberger Recommends "Self-Interest Through Delegation: An Additional Rationale for the Principal-Agent Relationship" by John Hamman, George Loewenstein, and Roberto Weber

Reiner Eichenberger

》 *Real-life behavior in situations where individuals can delegate their decisions to agents and where there are many action alternatives differs systematically from behavior in experiments with narrowly constrained action alternatives. This, however, does not mean that experiments are totally useless.*

The behavioral revolution in economics started in the late 1970s. Experimental evidence showed that real humans are not homines oeconomici: Real humans err systematically and behave impressively fairly. Shockingly, they do so in very simple games such as dictator and ultimatum games. Thus, human behavior cannot be explained by information cost, uncertainty, or complex strategies. It is simply anomalous.

In the 1980s, behavioral economists were convinced that behavioral insights would fundamentally change economics in due time. Today, we know that those economists were wrong. Of course, behavioral economics is well and alive; each year, a huge number of behavioral papers are published. But

R. Eichenberger (✉)
Economic and Financial Policy, University of Fribourg, Fribourg, Switzerland
e-mail: reiner.eichenberger@unifr.ch

© Springer Nature Switzerland AG 2019
B. S. Frey, C. A. Schaltegger (eds.), *21st Century Economics*,
https://doi.org/10.1007/978-3-030-17740-9_14

the effect on standard economics was minor. In the large majority of economic analyses, behavioral insights do not play a role. Why did the behavioral revolution fail?

When I was young, I also believed in the revolution. Actually, it was convincingly shown that anomalies also turn up under competition and in the behavior of experts. But in the late 1980s, I lost half of my belief when I realized that most anomalies do not affect the relative price effect. Thus, they are not a substitute for economics, but they remained an important complement. The second half of my belief faded away only in the 2000s. I learned that reality is not an experiment. In real life, there are two main reasons for individuals to behave as if they were homines oeconomici. This can be explained most easily by looking at dictator and ultimatum games.

First, fairness decreases dramatically if dictators, proposers, and responders get more action alternatives. Examples are experiments in which dictators can either keep their money, transfer it to the recipient, or buy a lottery with negative expectancy value (Felix Oberholzer-Gee and the author) and ultimatum games in which responders can react to unfair offers either by accepting them, rejecting them, or communicating their negative emotions to the proposers (Erte Xiao and Daniel Houser).

Second, fairness breaks down if humans delegate their choice to agents, that is, as soon as they are principals. Although they behave fairly if they act as dictators or proposers, they delegate their decisions to agents who promise to act in the fullest self-interest of the principal, and they require their agents to act in their fullest self-interest. Moreover, recipients and responders are less critical of agents who maximize the selfish utility of their principals than of principals who maximize their own selfish utility. All this is most elegantly shown and discussed by John Hamman, George Loewenstein, and Roberto Weber (2010). Although their experiments are only about delegation and fairness, it is most plausible that delegation also transforms other anomalies. In short, most people like to generously spend their money, but they do not like their agents to generously spend their money, and most people who regularly behave anomalously do not like their agents to behave anomalously.

This research has important implications: Real-life behavior in situations where individuals can delegate their decisions to agents and where there are many action alternatives differs systematically from behavior in experiments with narrowly constrained action alternatives. This, however, does not mean that experiments are useless. They are at least useful for analyzing the striking difference between human behavior in reality and in experiments.

Literature

Hamman, J., Loewenstein, G., & Weber, R. (2010). Self-interest through delegation: An additional rationale for the principal-agent relationship. *American Economic Review, 100*, 1826–1846.

Lars P. Feld Recommends "Happiness, Economy and Institutions" by Bruno S. Frey and Alois Stutzer

Lars P. Feld

>> *Frey and Stutzer make the real-life characteristics of individual decision-making explicit and show how this affects economic and political outcomes under different institutional settings.*

The title of this volume has inspired me to discuss a paper that has influenced my thinking very much. In this paper, Frey and Stutzer analyze factors that affect subjective well-being. They focus on institutional effects, in particular the impact of direct democracy, on well-being, using Swiss data. The size of the effect amounts to the happiness effect of a jump from the lowest- to the second lowest-income class. Interestingly, foreigners benefit less than the Swiss, such that an additional procedural utility occurs beyond pure income effects.

First, this paper has influenced my thinking because it is a nice complement of the literature on direct democracy. It contributed to the literature on direct democracy and public finances and on direct democracy and labor pro-

L. P. Feld (✉)
Albert-Ludwigs-University of Freiburg, Freiburg, Germany

Walter Eucken Institute, Freiburg, Germany
e-mail: feld@eucken.de

© Springer Nature Switzerland AG 2019
B. S. Frey, C. A. Schaltegger (eds.), *21st Century Economics*,
https://doi.org/10.1007/978-3-030-17740-9_15

ductivity, and I believe that the Frey and Stutzer paper was highly welcome to this line of thought.

Second, the paper has been highly influential on happiness research in economics. Together with the following papers by these authors, it triggered a wave of further studies. I have found this new perspective very important for scientific progress.

Third, this paper reflects Frey's research interests in an incomparable way. On the one side, he has contributed significantly to public choice and constitutional political economy. He has addressed many different research questions in these fields, among others a comparative analysis of institutions, to which this paper adds. On the other side, since his earlier works on anomalies in decision-making, Frey has contributed to psychological and behavioral economics. Again, he covers different aspects in this field and has focused on happiness research more recently. The Frey and Stutzer paper is one of his first papers in this area. Linking these two strands of research, constitutional and behavioral economics, this paper is exemplary and thus stands for the overall influence Frey has had on my economic thinking.

Fourth, there is an even broader perspective. I think that this paper addresses the missing link in the thinking of James M. Buchanan and Friedrich A. von Hayek and stands as an example as to how Frey's scientific work fills this gap. Buchanan received the Nobel Prize for his contractual and constitutional analyses of economic and political decision-making. He applied the economic model of human behavior to political decision-making and focused on constitutional rules to guide this behavior. Hayek was awarded the Nobel Prize for his analysis of the interdependence of economic, social, and institutional phenomena, in particular his ideas about decentralized subjective knowledge. In contrast to Buchanan, Hayek's view of individual decision-making contains fewer demanding prerequisites on individual rationality. He outlined these ideas in his *Sensory Order*, a book that has received more attention in recent decades than ever before. Hayek's *Sensory Order* anticipates several insights from behavioral economics. From this starting point, he outlines why rules rather than discretion should be dominant in economic policy. Both Buchanan and Hayek arrive at a rules-based approach to politics, but from different perspectives on individual rationality.

Frey, in contrast, makes the real-life characteristics of individual decision-making explicit and shows how this affects economic and political outcomes under different institutional settings. In this paper on happiness and institutions, the idea of procedural utility stands out, emphasizing that a proper working of institutions has preconditions beyond the narrow economic view.

Literature

Frey, B. S., & Stutzer, A. (2000). Happiness, economy and institutions. *Economic Journal, 110*, 918–938.

Reto Foellmi Recommends "Firms in International Trade" by Andrew B. Bernard, J. Bradford Jensen, Stephen J. Redding and Peter K. Schott

Reto Foellmi

> **》** *The findings of Bernard* et al. *show that the resilience to shocks and the ability to sustain inequalities are central elements for successful economies in the future. It is interesting to explore what characteristics in economics and policy help in attaining these goals.*

Since World War II, we have seen an ever-increasing amount of international exchange of goods, services, labour and capital. In politics and society alike, the potential effects of this phenomenon are eagerly discussed more than ever. However, knowledge is still scarce how this important feature of globalization affects the functioning of markets and firms on a smaller scale.

In a succinct and easy-to-read summary of their own and some other work, Bernard et al. (2007) highlight which actors actually trade. Maybe different to general views, trade is still a rare phenomenon. What is not too surprising is that only a small share of firms engage in exporting. In most OECD countries, less than 10% of firms are exporters. Even if we account for the fact that exporters are on average double as large as non-exporters, most workers are employed in

R. Foellmi (✉)
SIAW-HSG, University of St. Gallen, St. Gallen, Switzerland
e-mail: reto.foellmi@unisg.ch

© Springer Nature Switzerland AG 2019
B. S. Frey, C. A. Schaltegger (eds.), *21st Century Economics*,
https://doi.org/10.1007/978-3-030-17740-9_16

domestic-only firms. Controlling for different branches, exporters are always a minority even in export-oriented sectors like machinery or pharmaceuticals.

Comparing exporting and non-exporting firms, exporters are very different. On average, they are larger and much more productive, the latter holding true even if you control for size. Higher productivity is associated with the fact that exporters attract better-skilled workers and pay higher salaries. What I found most surprising is that inequality between firms is very pronounced amongst the group of exporters too. Bernard et al. document that international trade is extremely concentrated across exporting firms. In 2000, the top 1% of trading firms by value accounted for over 80% of the value of total trade. However, they employed only a share of 14% of all workers amongst exporters. Likely, concentration is currently more pronounced as a result of the winner-takes-all features of ICT technology.

This basic insight about firm structure bears an important implication on the effect of trade liberalization—or on the opposite—what could happen if trade barriers were rebuilt. Since firms are so different, integration in larger markets is likely to lead to large shifts in employment. The more productive, innovative firms will attract workers and potentially migrants. Less productive firms and sectors will shrink and possibly leave the market.

These findings by Bernard et al. link globalization with structural change. Consequently, we learn more about the interplay between trade, structural change and inequalities between individuals and firms. In the past, these issues played a minor role in economic science. To judge the feasibility of open markets, at least in democratic societies, it seems central to understand these phenomena better.

In my view, the ability of an economy to allow structural changes is central to sustained growth and—eventually—to maintaining a stable democracy with free markets. The big changes by new technologies and globalization force the economy to adapt at a high speed because the underlying firm and sectoral structure are crucially affected. On the opposite, growth prospects are doomed if a political process, such as capture by rent-seekers, tries to block these changes.

The findings of Bernard et al. have brought these arguments back to the table. Resilience to shocks and the ability to sustain inequalities are central elements for successful economies in the future. It is interesting to explore what characteristics in economics and policy help in attaining these goals.

Literature

Bernard, A. B., Jensen, J. B., Redding, S. J., & Schott, P. K. (2007). Firms in international trade. *Journal of Economic Perspectives, 21*(3), 105–130.

Nicolai J. Foss Recommends "Economics and Identity" by George A. Akerlof and Rachel E. Kranton

Nicolai J. Foss

>> *In spite of its obvious importance, it was not until the seminal 2000 Quarterly Journal of Economics article by Nobel laureate George Akerlof and Rachel Kranton on "Economics and Identity" that identity was placed directly on the agenda of economists.*

Social identity has entered the discourse of social scientists, pundits, and politicians to an extent that no one could have anticipated only about a decade ago. Thus, recent electoral events have strongly pointed to the importance of identity. For example, the 2016 Brexit UK election was at least partly a clash between the "anywheres" (i.e., people who by virtue of education, employment career, and general outlook identify less with a particular place and its community) and the "somewheres" (those who identify with specific places and their communities). Similarly, there is a case to be made that the outcome of the 2016 US presidential election was partly driven by some traditionally democratic workers shifting allegiance in response to the Democratic Party pursuing identity politics that alienated them.

N. J. Foss (✉)
Bocconi University, Milan, Italy
e-mail: nicolai.foss@unibocconi.it

© Springer Nature Switzerland AG 2019
B. S. Frey, C. A. Schaltegger (eds.), *21st Century Economics*,
https://doi.org/10.1007/978-3-030-17740-9_17

As social psychologists have argued for decades, parts of the self-concept, cognition, motivation, and behavior of individuals are derived from belonging to various groups. Humans may have been hardwired by evolution to form allegiance to potentially overlapping or nested groups and communities. Identity is at the heart of phenomena like mass movements, corporate culture, segregation, leadership, school choice, the supply of effort in organizations, and much else, and it informs the understanding of the supply of public goods and how norms constrain action and interaction.

In spite of its obvious importance, it was not until the seminal 2000 *Quarterly Journal of Economics* article by Nobel laureate George Akerlof and Rachel Kranton on "Economics and Identity" (see also their more popular summary in their 2010 book, *Identity Economics*) that identity was placed directly on the agenda of economists. (As Akerlof and Kranton suggest, however, other concepts that have been relatively prominent in economics, notably fairness and norms, often rest on a notion of identity). The basic idea is that identity can be represented by adding arguments to utility functions that capture how social group norms prescribe exemplary behavior (e.g., one argument for each group or category to which the individual belongs). Specifically, Akerlof and Kranton postulate the existence of "identity utility" and argue that actions—either those chosen by agents themselves or those of other agents with whom they engage in social comparison—that deviate from group norms lead to losses of such utility. To some extent, they argue, individuals can choose identities (also for others, e.g., parents choosing schools that shape the identities of their children). Akerlof and Kranton show how these ideas contribute to the analysis of highly topical issues, such as education, race, and poverty, the role gender in the labor market and in the home, and productivity and wages in organizations.

Although Akerlof and Kranton deserve unlimited kudos for putting identity into economics discourse, their use of existing scholarship on the subject is somewhat limited. They do not really discuss the dynamics of identities, how identities are nested, how they are partly activated by situational cues, how identifies influence cognition, or how different identities may be more or more less important at a given point of time. However, there is no reason why these ideas cannot also be modeled using the basic Akerlof and Kranton framework.

Literature

Akerlof, G. A., & Kranton, R. E. (2000). Economics and identity. *Quarterly Journal of Economics, 115*(3), 715–753.

Bruno S. Frey Recommends "Mindful Economics: The Production, Consumption, and Value of Beliefs" by Roland Bénabou and Jean Tirole

Bruno S. Frey

>> *Bénabou and Tirole's article opens up a significant new research program to be taken seriously by all those economists engaged in laboratory research— and far beyond.*

Behavioral economics has been a huge success in economics—despite its misnomer (economics has always been behavioral, so the field should aptly be called "economics and psychology" or "psychological economics"). Today, a large number of economists engage in laboratory experiments. Despite useful insights, it is often difficult to see what distinguishes them from psychology. All too often, the lab results are without further thought directly transferred to the aggregate societal level.

Bénabou and Tirole's article in the *Journal of Economic Perspectives* not only provides a most useful survey of recent insights of psychology but also makes a successful effort to integrate them into economics. They deal with heuristics and biases inconsistent with the standard homo oeconomicus such as over-

B. S. Frey (✉)
CREMA, Zurich, Switzerland

University of Basel, Basel, Switzerland
e-mail: bruno.frey@bsfrey.ch

© Springer Nature Switzerland AG 2019
B. S. Frey, C. A. Schaltegger (eds.), *21st Century Economics*,
https://doi.org/10.1007/978-3-030-17740-9_18

confidence, confirmation bias, distorted probability weighting, and other cognitive mistakes.

"Mindful Economics" is full of deep insights into "motivated beliefs and reasoning" and takes into account hundreds of recent contributions from economics and psychology, but also brain science, and political and organization theory. It stays close to empirical research and contributes economically relevant predictions. One, for instance, refers to information avoidance and asymmetric updating. The authors predict that individuals systematically fail to sufficiently update negative signals but are better capable of updating positive signals. This finding relates to the observation that a majority of people consider themselves to be above average, an effect which also applies to sophisticated persons.

The paper provides a number of other surprising observations. One is the effect of "stake-dependent beliefs" which are inconsistent with rational expectations and are the exact opposite of the much-heralded confirmation bias. The authors discuss, for instance, systematic departures from objective cognition. They may either be affective, where individuals make themselves or their future look better than they are in reality, or functional, where they help to achieve internal or external goals such as by influencing other persons. Another surprising finding is that our brains are involved in various processes of voluntary forgetting. This stands in contrast to the idea that if one wants to forget an incident, it becomes more vivid.

I welcome in particular that Bénabou and Tirole make a decisive and successful effort to look at the processes leading from individual motivated beliefs and reasoning to the consequences at the level of organizations and the economy. It could, for instance, be argued that systematic biases and mistakes are weeded out in markets characterized by perfect competition in economic or political markets. Alas, much of our world is far from being perfectly competitive, as the dominance of a few digital companies and of many authoritarian governments reveals. As a consequence, the environmental and institutional conditions strongly determine the benefits and costs arising in the aggregation process of psychological effects to aggregate outcomes. They must be taken into account in an effort to usefully introduce psychological insights to explain and shape economic affairs.

Bénabou and Tirole's article opens up a significant new research program to be taken seriously by all those economists engaged in laboratory research— and far beyond.

Literature

Bénabou, R., & Tirole, J. (2016). Mindful economics: The production, consumption, and value of beliefs. *Journal of Economic Perspectives, 30*(3), 141–164.

Jetta Frost Recommends "Collective Action and the Evolution of Social Norms" by Elinor Ostrom

Jetta Frost

» *Until now, economic theories of the firm have treated behaviour as postulated assumptions and described it as exogenously given. Accordingly, the content of firm members' preferences ultimately determines organizational governance. In fact, the effect of organizational governance is never immediate.*

Nowadays, more attention is paid to the collective aspect of organizations, namely, that interdependent chunks of activities, decisions, resources and knowledge are interlocked to form joint bundles of collective resources so that added value is created. To manage these bundles effectively, a firm needs members who are willing to engage in and contribute to collaborative activities. Nevertheless, firms, like political organizations and self-organized resource governance regimes, are vulnerable to the imminent danger of social dilemma situations. To govern collective action effectively therefore lies at the heart of the governance challenges of firms. However, until now, economic

J. Frost (✉)
Faculty of Business, Economics and Social Sciences, University of Hamburg, Hamburg, Germany
e-mail: Jetta.Frost@uni-hamburg.de

© Springer Nature Switzerland AG 2019
B. S. Frey, C. A. Schaltegger (eds.), *21st Century Economics*,
https://doi.org/10.1007/978-3-030-17740-9_19

theories of the firm have treated behaviour as postulated assumptions and described it as exogenously given. Accordingly, the content of firm members' preferences ultimately determines organizational governance. In fact, the effect of organizational governance is never immediate. The impact is reflected in the type of governance modes and design principles that influence the behaviour of actors striving towards collective action. It is precisely at this point that the focus should be shifted towards—and of course, where you should read and remember—the seminal work "Collective Action and the Evolution of Social Norms" by Elinor Ostrom, published in the *Journal of Economic Perspectives* in 2000.

Relying on an indirect evolutionary approach, Ostrom demonstrates a more optimistic understanding than the zero-contribution hypothesis dominating traditional notions of collective action. With a view to revising the theory of collective action, she raises the question of how potential cooperators signal to one another and can act as conditional cooperators, and she suggests considering multiple types of actors. She discusses laboratory experiments and field studies by drawing on evolutionary theory providing underpinnings for the propensity to cooperate based on the development and growth of social norms, such as fairness, trust and reciprocity. As shared understandings about actions that are essential, such norms have a certain staying power in encouraging cooperative behaviour.

Ostrom's research offers a more comprehensive approach, in which definitions of human behaviour are not assumed in an axiomatic manner, as they are in traditional economic theories of the firm. According to the latter, organizational governance results from placing strong emphasis on the notion of rational behaviour, which assumes a tendency to behave opportunistically on the part of the firm members. However, endogenous factors of influence are not considered although these forms of motivation can facilitate organizational learning processes and the evolution of social norms. Ostrom's work benefits research on organizational governance. It is to her credit that the active role of design principles in transforming behaviour can be taken into account. Applying her findings to organization governance in firms allows us to interpret preference patterns rather than merely treat them exogenously. By specifying design principles under which certain firm members' behaviour can be expected, a feasible solution can be found when it comes to resolving social dilemmas. Firm members facing a collective action problem would approach it with different intrinsic preferences over outcomes due to their predispositions towards social norms. The employment of organizational governance is therefore not simply the conclusion drawn from specific behavioural assumptions; it can also bring about certain behavioural effects: it makes it possible to reinforce conditional cooperation.

Literature

Ostrom, E. (2000). Collective action and the evolution of social norms. *Journal of Economic Perspectives, 14*(3), 137–158.

Clemens Fuest Recommends "Yes, Economics Is a Science" by Raj Chetty

Clemens Fuest

>> *Raj Chetty's article is very helpful because he clearly explains what we can expect from economic research. In his view, economics is a science because economists develop precise hypotheses and test them empirically using data.*

Every economist who participates in debates about economic policy knows that, among "ordinary people," the reputation of economics as a science is not great. The fact that economists often disagree is cited by many as proof that economic research is unreliable. For instance, the difference between "hawks" and "doves" in monetary or fiscal policy is an issue that regularly hits the headlines. Interestingly, most people know from their own experience that doctors often come up with different diagnoses for the same patient. But that does not make many people doubt that medicine is a science.

The debate over the status of economics as a science is important because the quality of economic policy decisions depends on whether or not they are based

C. Fuest (✉)
ifo Institute, Munich, Germany

Center of Economic Studies, Ludwig-Maximilians-University of Munich, Munich, Germany
e-mail: fuest@ifo.de

© Springer Nature Switzerland AG 2019
B. S. Frey, C. A. Schaltegger (eds.), *21st Century Economics*,
https://doi.org/10.1007/978-3-030-17740-9_20

57

on sound economic reasoning. Raj Chetty's article is very helpful because he clearly explains what we can expect from economic research. In his view, economics is a science because economists develop precise hypotheses and test them empirically using data. Of course, checking whether economic theories are compatible with what we observe is complicated by the fact that scope for running experiments is limited. This also holds true for medicine. We do not want to cause recessions just to understand what their effects are, and doctors do not produce epidemics just to study their effects and how they can be stopped. But we have developed methods to extract and interpret information from policy changes and economic events like recessions or booms. Credible empirical evidence is easier to produce for some issues than for others. For instance, measuring whether firms invest more if corporate taxes fall, as suggested by economic theory, works relatively well thanks to the availability of large datasets with information on thousands of individual firms. By contrast, big-picture questions like "how does debt-financed public spending affect economic growth" are more difficult to analyze empirically. The number of countries we observe is much smaller than the number of firms, and the direction of causality between fiscal policy and growth is less clear. Other disciplines including medicine face similar issues: The impact of taking aspirin on the composition of the blood is relatively easy to measure, but broader questions like what makes people remain healthy until they are old are harder to answer.

So far, we have only discussed research about causal relationships between economic variables. Here, differences among experts may stem from different views on data quality, suitable measurement techniques, or the interpretation of results. When it comes to policy questions, differences among economists may reflect the fact that economists use different criteria for the objectives of economic policy. These criteria, including the implied value judgments, are not always made explicit. But again, disagreement is no proof that there is anything "unscientific" in these debates.

More generally, differences in views may well reflect the individual biases and prejudices of academics, who are no more objective than other people. But as Karl Popper famously pointed out, "It is completely erroneous to assume that the objectivity of a science depends upon the objectivity of the scientist…the objectivity of science is not a matter for the individual scientist, but rather the social result of mutual criticism."

Literature

Chetty, R. (2013, October 13). Yes, economics is a science. New York Times Op-ed. https://www.nytimes.com/2013/10/21/opinion/yes-economics-is-a-science.html

Allan Guggenbühl Recommends "Storytelling Animal. How Stories Make Us Human" by Jonathan Gottschall

Allan Guggenbühl

>> *The economy thrives when we are capable of combining services with stories. In order to persuade us, they need to be performed, authentic and not just a marketing strategy.*

We are entering a restaurant in Lviv, Ukraine. The premises can be reached by descending a narrow spiral staircase. Having reached the bottom, the customers are asked to advance through a tunnel—in pitch darkness. The passage leads to a dining room. There, dressed as miners, waiters welcome the courageous intruders. A complimentary coffee is offered, which is prepared with the help of a blaze exuding from pistol-like flame-throwers. The setting allows customers to experience the hard lives of coal miners before finally enjoying a drink and a bite. Most likely, towns in Europe would refuse to permit such premises. Safety regulations, sanitary standards, and obligatory guidelines would make it impossible to open such a place. In Ukraine, where many rules are unclear and the state has a less tight grip on entrepreneurial enterprises, such a challenging eating place is possible.

A. Guggenbühl (✉)
Institute for Conflict Management and Mythodrama (IKM), Zurich, Switzerland
e-mail: algugg@hispeed.ch; http://www.ikm.ch

© Springer Nature Switzerland AG 2019
B. S. Frey, C. A. Schaltegger (eds.), *21st Century Economics*,
https://doi.org/10.1007/978-3-030-17740-9_21

The economy is based on innovation. People are willing to buy new products or use services when they feel the quality of their lives will improve or a need is satisfied. With technical products, this is obvious: the new iPhone has more storage space, or the automatic lawn mower frees us from tedious gardening. With services, which are offered by humans and include personal interaction, it is more complicated; quality is not the core argument. Why should eating out in a newly opened restaurant be better than the places one already visits? In order to attract new customers, the service must promise *more* than just an improvement of quality. The service, be it food, counselling, therapy, or self-enhancement, must *fascinate* possible customers. In contrast to other mammals, humans wish to transfer themselves occasionally mentally into other worlds and situations. They have the ability to imagine themselves to be somebody else and be somewhere else. We humans can envisage how life was in the middle ages or how it is to own a yacht in the Caribbean. The images and scenarios in our head are often very powerful. They lead us to change our lives and accept risks. Our imagination is evoked with the help of *stories*, which transport us into extraordinary situations. This is why narratives from the past, adventure stories, and stories of hardship and scandals excite us. They allow us to participate in scenarios that exist in our heads but that we are unable or unwilling to experience personally. The economy thrives when we are capable of combining services with stories. In order to persuade us, they need to be performed, authentic and not just a marketing strategy.

The economy needs to be regulated in order to protect us from being cheated or having an accident. Regulations impose *norms*, which are based on the experiences and competences of the respective professional association and political demands. The aim is the prevention of the exceptional and the reduction of risks. Professional societies want to keep everything under control, define how a job is done, and are inclined to be politically correct. The snag is that too many rules block imagination. People dread normality. They yearn for stories that connect with the exceptional. If a service is too regulated, new stories are excluded. The danger is that services are unable to connect with an upcoming story. In order to prosper, societies need to allow entrepreneurs to pursue unprecedented ideas and allow experiments that connect to the stories people are fascinated by. These might be politically incorrect and shadowy and involve risks. The economy prospers with the help of new stories. The restaurant in Lviv was based on a powerful story about the dire lives of coal miners. Perhaps this is only possible in a semi-chaotic society, like currently the Ukraine.

Literature

Gottschall, J. (2012). *Storytelling animal. How stories make us human.* New York: Mariner.

Jochen Hartwig Recommends "In It Together: Why Less Inequality Benefits All" by OECD

Jochen Hartwig

Income inequality is "the defining challenge of our time," former US President Barack Obama said in a speech in December 2013. Undoubtedly, the financial crisis and the sluggish recovery in its aftermath have increased attention to rising inequality. Against this backdrop, the OECD published a report titled *In It Together – Why Less Inequality Benefits All* in 2015. This is a text you should read and remember because it thoroughly points out why inequality is harmful and what can be done to reduce it. It addresses inequality trends with a special focus on the recent period of crisis and fiscal consolidation; distinguishes between income and wealth inequalities; analyses how rising nonstandard work, job polarization, and changes in women's employment have impacted inequality; and discusses the leeway for emerging economies to reduce it.

The most important findings of the report, however, are those on the nexus between inequality and economic growth. Using panel data for 31 OECD countries over the period 1970–2010 and applying the System-GMM estimator to address reverse causality, per capita GDP growth over 5-year intervals is regressed on the log of per capita GDP at the beginning of the 5-year period, the log of the market Gini coefficient (which measures inequality in a country before redistribution through taxes and transfers) at the beginning of the 5-year period or the log of the net Gini coefficient (which measures inequality

J. Hartwig (✉)
Faculty of Economics and Business Administration, Technische Universität Chemnitz, Chemnitz, Germany
e-mail: jochen.hartwig@wirtschaft.tu-chemnitz.de

© Springer Nature Switzerland AG 2019
B. S. Frey, C. A. Schaltegger (eds.), *21st Century Economics*,
https://doi.org/10.1007/978-3-030-17740-9_22

after redistribution), and the extent of redistribution (i.e., the difference between the market and net Ginis). Control variables for human and physical capital accumulation are added.

The report finds a significantly negative impact of net inequality on economic growth. A drop in the net Gini coefficient—which means a reduction in inequality—by 1 base point would raise per capita GDP growth by 0.15 percentage points per year over the next 5 years. Poor households' inability to invest in their human capital is the main transmission mechanism between inequality and growth. The coefficient on the redistribution variable, on the other hand, is found to be insignificant, which means that, contrary to widespread belief, redistribution is not harmful to growth. "Taken together, these results suggest that inequality in disposable incomes is bad for growth, and that redistribution is, at worst, neutral to growth," the report concludes.

By showing that less inequality would benefit us all by raising the rate of growth of the economy, the OECD has rendered the world a service. Of course, critics (like the Council of Economic Experts advising the German government) have questioned the robustness of the empirical results; and the policies the OECD recommends to tackle inequality in *In It Together* are less ambitious than those suggested by the late Sir Anthony Atkinson. Nevertheless, when an international organization like the OECD throws its weight behind the cause of reducing inequality, a change for the better could be in the offing. Arthur Cecil Pigou once opined that "[i]f it were not for the hope that a scientific study of man's social actions may lead ... to practical results in social improvement, I should myself ... regard the time devoted to that study as misspent." In crafting *In It Together*, the OECD did not misspend its time. Reading this study will not waste yours.

Literature

OECD. (2015). *In it together: Why less inequality benefits all*. Paris: OECD Publishing.

Jürg Helbling Recommends "Capital in the Twenty-First Century" by Thomas Piketty

Jürg Helbling

>> *A high inequality of wealth has several conse-quences, for it will not only slow economic growth but also endanger democracy and threaten social stability.*

Piketty puts economic inequality back on the agenda not only of economic debate but also of public discussion. Whereas mainstream economics considers budget restrictions for households and firms and emphasizes the importance of private property rights, Piketty addresses the unequal distribution of wealth and its consequences for economic growth and social stability. For him, economics is a social science—or political economy—that seeks to contribute to an understanding not only of the current problems but also of the history of industrial-capitalist societies by taking political structures and processes into account as well. Piketty uses a historical and statistical approach to examine the development of the unequal distribution of wealth in Europe and the United States since the late eighteenth century.

J. Helbling (✉)
Kultur-und Sozialwissenschaftliche Fakultät, Ethnologisches Seminar, University of Lucerne, Lucerne, Switzerland
e-mail: Juerg.Helbling@unilu.ch

© Springer Nature Switzerland AG 2019
B. S. Frey, C. A. Schaltegger (eds.), *21st Century Economics*,
https://doi.org/10.1007/978-3-030-17740-9_23

65

By using an impressive mass and a wide range of statistical data, Piketty demonstrates that the inequality of wealth increased in the long nineteenth century with a peak at the eve of World War I, after which it started to decrease, particularly in the course of the world economic crises in the 1930s and during World War II and, due to progressive taxation of capital and income, remained low until 1975. It was only in the 1970s and 1980s that inequality of wealth distribution started to increase again.

Wealth consists of income and capital (property). Income stems from labor (wages and salaries) and from capital (profits, dividends, interest, rents, and other income from capital ownership). Capital (K), or property, comprises bonds and shares as well as means of production and real estate. The total income (Y) is the value of goods produced and sold during a year (GDP). Total capital is the result of the accumulation of income in previous years. The higher the inequality of income is, the greater the capital formation in the highest decile of the income strata will be. Consumption reduces wealth; saving increases it. Capital can be invested and accumulated. Piketty measures the unequal distribution of wealth as the capital/income rate multiplied by the rate of return on capital ($K/Y * r$). For the share of capital in total income to remain constant, the return on capital (r) must be equal to the rate of economic growth (g). According to Piketty, r tends to grow faster than g in the history of capitalism, with a growing inequality as a consequence. But r may also grow slower than g with the inequality in wealth distribution decreasing, as was the case between World War I and the late 1970s.

As long as the rate of return on capital exceeds the rate of growth, the income and wealth of the rich will grow faster than the typical income from work. A high inequality of wealth has several consequences, for it will not only slow economic growth but also endanger democracy and threaten social stability. The concentration of capital is an endogenous feature of capitalism without state intervention. Only the tax policy of the state can create a counterweight to this. Taxation of inheritance and of high income strata—as well as the skillful use of tax revenues—will thus reduce the unequal distribution of wealth as well as promote economic growth, strengthen democracy, and contribute to social stability.

Literature

Piketty, T. (2013). *Le Capital au XXIe siècle*. Editions du Seuil, Paris. (*Capital in the 21st Century*). Cambridge MA: The Belknap Press of Harvard University Press, 2014.

Sir David F. Hendry Recommends "An Analysis of the Indicator Saturation Estimator as a Robust Regression Estimator" by Søren Johansen and Bent Nielsen

Sir David F. Hendry

>> *Søren Johansen and Bent Nielsen opened a door to tackling outliers and shifts: indicator saturation is most definitely an idea you should remember— and apply.*

Economies are buffeted by many forces—financial and oil crises, wars and natural catastrophes—but much economic analysis concerns equilibrium states. Empirical modelling not accounting for shifts in the distributions of the variables risks reaching misleading conclusions by wrongly attributing explanations, as well as from non-constant parameters. While dates of the Great Depression, oil and financial crises and major wars are known ex post, the durations and magnitudes of their impacts on economies are almost never known. Time-series researchers must neutralize the impacts of shifts and outliers on estimates of parameters of interest.

Søren Johansen and Bent Nielsen (JN) formalize impulse-indicator saturation (IIS) analysis to do so. An impulse indicator is unity for 1 observation and zero elsewhere so delivers a zero residual at that observation. T indicators are created for T observations, so the sample is 'saturated'. Half ($T/2$) the indicators are entered in the model in turn as the simplest way to analyse

S. D. F. Hendry (✉)
Nuffield College, University of Oxford, Oxford, UK
e-mail: david.hendry@nuffield.ox.ac.uk

© Springer Nature Switzerland AG 2019
B. S. Frey, C. A. Schaltegger (eds.), *21st Century Economics*,
https://doi.org/10.1007/978-3-030-17740-9_24

67

IIS. Including each $T/2$ indicators provides unbiased model estimates from the other half, and discrepancies relative to that half can be tested for significance. Reverse halves then combine selected indicators.

IIS is related to many well-known statistical approaches, including recursive estimation, rolling regressions, dropping observations for 'discrepant' periods such as wars, etc. As the variation in discrepant periods can break collinearities, much can be learned by applying IIS instead. The Chow test for parameter constancy is a special case of IIS, so IIS can detect shifts as well as outliers. IIS on instrumental variables allows checking the instrument equations for outliers and shifts and testing the equation of interest for invariance. IIS has affinities to robust statistics: JN relate it to Huber's skip estimator.

JN establish the statistical properties of IIS for no outliers for stationary, trend stationary and unit-root relations. Despite using more variables plus indicators than observations, the asymptotic distributions reveal IIS as nearly the statistical equivalent of a free lunch. For stationarity with symmetric errors, the limiting estimator distribution for the parameters of interest converges to the population parameter at $\sqrt{T}$ and is normal. The variance is larger than conventional: around 1% larger for a 1% significance level. If the significance level is $1/T$, one irrelevant impulse indicator will be retained on average by chance. Think of it: IIS checks T impulse indicators for their significance almost costlessly when not needed, yet tests for an unknown number of outliers of unknown magnitudes and signs, not knowing where in the data they occurred!

Johansen and Nielsen's analysis is more complicated when there are trends or unit roots, involving different normalizations than $\sqrt{T}$ and different limiting distributions for integrated processes but delivers similar implications. Many generalizations have since been proposed, including step-, trend-, designer- and multiple-indicator saturation. Software implements these by inspecting many divisions into blocks and searching many paths: selection of indicators can be joint with selecting other regressors. Applications of indicator saturation include dendrochronology, volcanology, climatology and economics.

Søren Johansen and Bent Nielsen opened a door to tackling outliers and shifts: indicator saturation is most definitely an idea you should remember—and apply.

Literature

Johansen, S., & Nielsen, B. (2009). An analysis of the indicator saturation estimator as a robust regression estimator. In J. L. Castle & N. Shephard (Eds.), *The methodology and practice of econometrics* (pp. 1–36). Oxford: Oxford University Press.

Gerard Hertig Recommends "Legal Origins" by Edward L. Glaeser and Andrei Shleifer

Gerard Hertig

>> *Clearly, culture, politics, and religion are likely to influence the legal regime and its economic impact. The crucial issue, however, is whether legal origin is a proxy for merely one or for several of these factors.*

In a series of contributions spanning more than a decade, Andrei Shleifer and various co-authors have introduced a path-breaking approach to business law issues that is both more "scientific" and pluri-disciplinary than what the legal and academic profession had previously generated.

It all started with a set of corporate governance pieces during the 1997–2000 period, which brought financial and data-based analyses to the dusty world of comparative law. This work revolutionized scholarly research around the globe by forcing any respected contributor to take into account the functional and historical drivers of corporate and financial regulation.

Two more recent contributions, one on Legal Origins (2002) and the other on Courts (2003), have more fundamentally changed the way to approach regulatory issues, via the *law and finance* approach. The focus here is on the

G. Hertig (✉)
ETH Zurich, Zurich, Switzerland
e-mail: ghertig@ethz.ch

© Springer Nature Switzerland AG 2019
B. S. Frey, C. A. Schaltegger (eds.), *21st Century Economics*,
https://doi.org/10.1007/978-3-030-17740-9_25

former contribution, published in the *Quarterly Journal of Economics* (volume 117, 1193–1229) and co-authored with Edward Glaeser.

Legal Origins appropriately starts with a historical observation that the laws of many countries are heavily influenced by either English common law or French civil law.

It then points out that common law is generally associated with judge-made law and civil law with statutory regulation, the former being implemented by lay judges and the latter by professional judges. For the authors, this is due to local magnates being originally more powerful in France (thus having to be kept under control by state-employed judges) and weaker in England (allowing for juries). They thus argue that France chose to rely on state-employed judges because of local feudal lords being too powerful, whereas juries were less vulnerable in England due to local magnates being weaker.

Based on these observations, the authors model codification as an efficient attempt by the sovereign to control judges.

This model approach and the empirical studies it generated have not proven popular among social scientists. Historians, lawyers, and political economists have challenged the comparative validity of the approach. For some, "transplanted" institutions are unlikely to remain stable over time, which makes a civil vs common law comparison overly simplistic. For others, culture, politics, and religion have more explanatory power than belonging to a specific legal tradition.

These criticisms are not without merit, as evidenced by Shleifer et al. having devoted significant attention to them. Clearly, culture, politics, and religion are likely to influence the legal regime and its economic impact. The crucial issue, however, is whether legal origin is a proxy for merely one or for several of these factors.

Conceptually, one can deal with this question by measuring differences in legal regime across countries and identifying whether they (1) are attributable to legal origins and (2) matter in terms of economic and social outcomes. The irony here is that to credibly do so, one has to use the very approach pioneered by Shleifer et al.: to develop a robust model and to gather a very large data set.

In short, Shleifer et al. have set the bar. Those who doubt the validity of their approach and/or conclusions must now operate at the same level. Early results show that critics have a point; whether they will debunk the approach and its conclusions is a much more open question.

Literature

Glaeser, E. L., & Shleifer, A. (2002). Legal origins. *Quarterly Journal of Economics, 117*, 1193–1229.

Bruno Heyndels Recommends "Gender Quotas and the Crisis of the Mediocre Man: Theory and Evidence from Sweden" by Timothy Besley, Olle Folke, Torsten Persson, and Johanna Rickne

Bruno Heyndels

» *In their 2017 article, Besley, Folke, Persson, and Rickne show how constraining political leaders in their choice and ordering of candidates may increase—not decrease—the general competence level of representatives.*

Some things we, economists, do not like. Maybe because we were taught to dislike them. Maybe because that is who we are. It seems like some things *should* be disliked. Political incorrectness may be one of these. We tend to dislike "should." Among economists, gender quotas in politics tend not to be liked. The meritocratic critique is that competence, not sex, should form the basis of political representation. Imposing more female representation would lead to less competent representatives and inferior policies. The claim is that constraining choices has rarely made the world a better place.

We prefer having competent politicians as they tend to better serve our interests. List systems of proportional representation are a common way of political selection. In such systems, party leaderships present preselected pools

B. Heyndels (✉)
Department of Applied Economics, Vrije Universiteit Brussel (VUB),
Brussels, Belgium
e-mail: Bruno.Heyndels@vub.be

© Springer Nature Switzerland AG 2019
B. S. Frey, C. A. Schaltegger (eds.), *21st Century Economics*,
https://doi.org/10.1007/978-3-030-17740-9_26

of candidates to the electorate. In their 2017 article, Besley, Folke, Persson, and Rickne show how constraining political leaders in their choice and ordering of candidates may increase—not decrease—the general competence level of representatives.

The basic idea in their article is simple. On the one hand, leaders have an incentive to select competent candidates as these increase their parties' popularity. On the other hand, they have an incentive to select mediocre candidates as these are less threatening for the leaders' own positions. As a result, the selection of candidates will reflect the leaders' own level of competence. Highly competent party leaders select competent followers. Mediocre leaders do not. They will not want to take the risk of losing their position to competent newcomers. The idea is familiar to anyone exposed to institutions where competition is not perfect—that is, *any* institution, private or public.

The authors demonstrate the effectiveness of zipper quotas, which require that no two successive candidates on a party list may be of identical sex. That such quotas are effective in selecting more female representatives is no surprise in a Swedish context of closed lists at the time. More interestingly, the authors show how introducing zipper quotas did not affect the quality of female representatives, thus contradicting the meritocratic critique, and increased the quality of male representatives. The driving mechanism was the resignation of mediocre male candidates.

Why should we remember these findings? First of all, they document that gender discrimination is not just a grandmother's tale. In #MeToo times, this deserves recognition if only because it illustrates the tension between politically correct words, the corresponding beliefs, and actual human behavior. Second, they illustrate how mediocrity reproduces itself if not administered carefully. That this may be the case because of mediocre leaders defending their own positions is an interesting insight. Looking at the world around us, most of us could name examples of competence seemingly being overlooked on purpose. Finally, Besley et al. not only point to the mediocre leaders' rationality of disregarding competence; they also show how competition may resolve the conundrum. They remind us of what we have known since Adam Smith: competition works. Constraining choice sometimes does make the world a better place.

Literature

Besley, T., Folke, O., Persson, T., & Rickne, J. (2017). Gender quotas and the crisis of the Mediocre Man: Theory and evidence from Sweden. *American Economic Review, 107*(8), 2204–2242.

David Iselin Recommends "The Superiority of Economists" by Marion Fourcade, Etienne Ollion, and Yann Algan

David Iselin

>> *The fine work of Fourcade and her colleagues helps place our field in the wider context of the social sciences.*

In 2015, Marion Fourcade, Etienne Ollion, and Yann Algan published an article in the *Journal of Economic Perspectives* that sheds light on economics in an unconventional way: The authors give a sociological perspective on the economics profession. They show how economists found their way to the top of the social sciences and how this reflects back into their self-perception. It may seem odd to include a sociological analysis of economics in an anthology of the most important—though personally colored—economic publications written in the last 20 years, but it is the fine work of Fourcade and her colleagues that helps place our field in the wider context of the social sciences.

Although the financial crisis has disenchanted economists' standing somewhat, they still come out at the top in the pecking order of social sciences. At least that is what many economists think. In surveys, economists do not shy away from agreeing with the statement "economics is the most scientific of the social sciences" in large numbers. The "market" seems to confirm the

D. Iselin (✉)
Berne Historical Museum, Berne, Switzerland
e-mail: david.iselin@bhm.ch

© Springer Nature Switzerland AG 2019
B. S. Frey, C. A. Schaltegger (eds.), *21st Century Economics*,
https://doi.org/10.1007/978-3-030-17740-9_27

"native's judgment about the higher status of economists": Economists are the only social scientists who can win a Nobel Prize, they command some of the highest levels of compensation in arts and science faculties, and they earn more than physicists and mathematicians. Unlike many academics in the theoretical sciences and humanities, economists have easier access to income from consulting fees, private investment, and partnerships as well as membership in corporate boards.

This combination of a much better financial position and the discipline's emphasis on mastering quantitative reasoning stands behind the sometimes dismissive attitude of economists toward the other, less formal social sciences, as Fourcade et al. note. Other reasons for the distant relations to their social brethren and sisters lie in the different social composition. Economics is a relatively insular field compared to other social sciences. An examination of interdisciplinary citations in flagship journals shows that articles in the *American Economic Review* cite five times fewer articles from the *American Political Science Review* than the other way around. Furthermore, the hierarchies are more pronounced, and economics has been male-dominated for many years. Economists also adore rankings and clear orderings, fostering the pecking order within the field.

One could argue that the relatively homogenous attitude of economists about what constitutes good work and how it is done advances the field, but that is not the main point here. The social sciences have a common heritage, yet the hyper-specialization has widened the gap between the different branches. This would be rather irrelevant if it did not coincide with a growing distance between economists and the larger public. Economists' general mission is to maximize the welfare of ordinary people. The world has changed a lot in the last 20 years under the influence of their mission. They have successfully disseminated their expertise on public policy, institutions, and entire countries. However, if their "fix-it" culture is perceived as aloof, economists will not be able to convince their colleagues from sociology and political science nor the democratic voter of their smart solutions. This is of relevance in highly contested times.

Literature

Fourcade, M., Ollion, E., & Algan, Y. (2015). The superiority of economists. *Journal of Economic Perspectives, 29*(1), 89–114. https://doi.org/10.1257/jep.29.1.89.

Beat Kappeler Recommends "Beyond the Keynesian Endpoint: Crushed by Credit and Deceived by Debt – How to Revive the Global Economy" by Tony Crescenzi

Beat Kappeler

>> *Today, the public doesn't ask for sound policies, as Crescenzi expected in 2011, but it elects and approves political coalitions and their budgets in even greater disequilibrium. The sticky wages and prices of Keynes have mutated into sticky expenditures, sticky deficits, and sticky monetary balances.*

Demand management by way of additional public spending is obsolete, if private and public debt levels are such that they must be reduced. This deleveraging will pull the marginal propensity to consume into reverse. It will be way below the assumptions of Keynesians and their multiplicator. Public spending therefore cannot be increased in order to reduce unemployment and foster growth, even less so as the public debt must be reduced in the first place. Shifting the ills of the private sector to the public sector, as practised after the financial crisis, is not possible any more. There are now overleveraged societies.

Even though developed countries never defaulted in the last decades or centuries, it is a fallacy to believe that new public debt can be issued as in the past 30 years. This is the Keynesian endpoint.

B. Kappeler (✉)
Hinterkappelen, Switzerland

© Springer Nature Switzerland AG 2019
B. S. Frey, C. A. Schaltegger (eds.), *21st Century Economics*,
https://doi.org/10.1007/978-3-030-17740-9_28

Writing in 2011, Crescenzi would indulge in "responsible irresponsible expansionary policies" by monetary easing in order to reduce the risk of deflation and restore the rate of inflation to around 2%.

For investment purposes, this would nevertheless produce new and unwelcome outcomes, such as steep yield curves, excess capacities in the economy with a risk of deflation, low interest volatility, and tighter credit spreads.

If Keynesian receipts were applied through these measures, the programs would be perceived by investors as promising too much. The public sector would not be trusted and could not raise money, currency devaluations would have to happen because of high inflation rates and high interest rates, and low economic returns would ensue.

Instead, Crescenzi intended to mend the Keynesian endpoint by a zero primary balance in the public accounts, by burden sharing through cutting entitlement spending, by a devaluation at the cost of the trading partners, by monetary transfers from other nations, and by haircuts of bond holders.

Rather a path of Austrian economics should be engaged, with emphasis not on consumption but on investment, this having a higher multiplier. Free trade agreements and budget rules should be added.

In 2011, these ideas were a sensible way out of the crisis. But since then the central banks have pushed the monetary "irresponsibility" to levels never seen before, by the way of quantitative easing under continually changing "remits." If ever rational expectations were influential as opposed to abstract models, today they have merged with monetary policies to a degree where any change, any deviation must cause panics and reverse, especially in the Euroregion. The loop of expectations is mutual between the central banks, the states and investors. The monetized indebtedness there, in the USA and in Japan, has veered even more to the Keynesian endpoint. At this stage, 2018, however, the public doesn't ask for sound policies, as Crescenzi expected in 2011, but it elects and approves political coalitions, and their budgets in even greater disequilibrium, in the USA, in Southern Europe, and in Japan. The sticky wages and prices of Keynes have mutated into sticky expenditures, sticky deficits, and sticky monetary balances. These monetary and budgetary policies are without a proven theoretical basis. The practitioners' view seems much more pertinent. And he warned that tail risks come suddenly, not incrementally.

Literature

Crescenzi, T. (2011). *Beyond the Keynesian endpoint: Crushed by credit and deceived by debt—how to revive the global economy*. New Jersey: Pearson.

Martin Killias Recommends "Crime and Everyday Life" by Marcus Felson and Rachel Boba

Martin Killias

>> *Who actually discovered the role of situational factors? After Aristotle, long forgotten, the man who first came up with this approach was Leslie T. Wilkins during and following WWII. Perhaps the most comprehensive and groundbreaking analysis nowadays is Marcus Felson and Rachel Boba's* Crime and Everyday Life.

You remember the times when, walking the streets, we regularly had to watch the ground in order not to march into what a dog might have left on the sidewalk? Many cities enacted regulations providing for fines or other punishment to deter careless dog owners. Nowadays, streets are clean, even in countries where the problem used to be a real nuisance. How did this come about? It was the invention of small plastic sacks that allowed dog owners to collect from the ground whatever their darling had left over and to dispose of it in a special litter box nearby. No other feasible measure might have achieved such success, at least not at acceptable costs.

M. Killias (✉)
Prof. em., Criminal Law, Criminal Procedure Law and Criminology, Universities of Zurich, St. Gallen, Lausanne, Switzerland
e-mail: martin.killias@unisg.ch

© Springer Nature Switzerland AG 2019
B. S. Frey, C. A. Schaltegger (eds.), *21st Century Economics*,
https://doi.org/10.1007/978-3-030-17740-9_29

What can we learn from this? First, situations in which humans act are more important than so-called human factors, including psychological profiles, past traumata, or deterrence-based threats. Motivation, as important as it may be, will only become manifest as long as the environment allows people to act out what they may have in their "hearts." Ironically, psychology, criminology, and many other human sciences have long focused exclusively on the reasons for human decisions, the ability of control of impulses, or the effects of traumata and other factors on all sorts of psychological disturbances and pathologies. This is not to argue that such aspects are unimportant. However, in order to prevent individual pathologies from becoming manifest in everyday interactions, changing environmental or situational factors regularly proves to be far easier than any attempts at changing human character.

Interestingly, the idea that problems might be solved or at least reduced without any moral improvement, or without addressing the "root" causes, continues to meet reservation from many psychologists, psychiatrists, and clergymen. From this point of view, it is more than remarkable that the recent special issue of *Psychology of Violence* (Ed. Sherry Hamby) is entirely devoted to situational factors of violence. Obviously, the decisive role of situations should not be seen as a "threat" by specialists of treatment but as a great opportunity to bring therapeutic approaches to work. Nobody would predict treatment of alcohol dependency to be successful as long as the patient continues to work as a barkeeper.

Trivial as it may be, the role of situations has long failed to be recognized. Why did crime increase during the decades following World War II? Why did it decline after the millennium in most Western countries? The simplest and most parsimonious explanation is the increasing opportunities to steal, to rob, and to deal in drugs during the second half of the last century and the spreading of security technologies at all levels of everyday life over the last 20 years. As the example of dogs illustrates, these innovations are not only "repressive" but often include opening access to acceptable solutions for people in trouble, from dog owners to applicants to government officials (bribing only if efficient and rapid services are unavailable) and heroin-dependent addicts who can be treated with opiates in special ambulant clinics.

Who actually discovered the role of situational factors? After Aristotle, long forgotten, the man who first came up with this approach was Leslie T. Wilkins during and following WWII. Perhaps the most comprehensive and groundbreaking analysis nowadays is Marcus Felson and Rachel Boba's *Crime and Everyday Life*, 4th edition (Sage 2010).

Literature

Felson, M., & Boba, R. (2010). *Crime and everyday life* (4th ed.). New York: Sage.

Hartmut Kliemt Recommends "Violence and Social Orders" by Douglass C. North, John Joseph Wallis, and Barry R. Weingast

Hartmut Kliemt

>> *Though Violence and Social Orders cannot explain how the anomaly of the great open-access society can arise and sustain itself, it makes it entirely clear that the private contract society is a political creation through and through. If it comes to the wealth of nations, it's politics—and not the economy—stupid! A timely reminder indeed!*

Violence and Social Orders, *VSO* henceforth, reminds economists that the free markets of Western open-access societies that extend "stability of possession, its transference by consent and the execution of promises" (Humean "natural law") to large numbers of citizens are political institutions. In a world in which the use of violence in furthering the interests of particular groups is always an option, the nonpartisan enforcement and prevalence of the legal conventions of natural law that are constitutive of the private contract society is a truly astonishing phenomenon: real politics creates a non-political sphere.

It would be a major accomplishment of political economy if it could explain in terms of corroborated law-like regularities how an open-access society can

H. Kliemt (✉)
VWL VI (Behavioral and Institutional Economics), Justus Liebig University, Giessen, Germany

© Springer Nature Switzerland AG 2019
B. S. Frey, C. A. Schaltegger (eds.), *21st Century Economics*,
https://doi.org/10.1007/978-3-030-17740-9_30

come about and can sustain itself through time. Yet, as *VSO* acknowledges, political economists are still in a position akin to that of medical doctors before the ascent of evidence-based medicine: They can describe the open-access society as a positive "syndrome" but cannot provide evidence-based technological advice on how to bring it about and to sustain it.

Contrary to a medical syndrome (as a negative deviation from a natural state of health), the open-access societies that have emerged in Europe and North America since 1814 form "unnatural" positive deviations from what is aptly called a "natural *state*" in *VSO*. The "natural *state*"—rather than the fictitious anarchical state of nature—is the organizational alternative with which an open-access society must be compared. This natural state is a governance organization which is sustained in the shadow of violence as an equilibrium among privilege-seeking groups or coalitions. To sustain it requires a continuous adjustment of privileges (rents) to the underlying power structure. Thereby, violence may be confined to the threat of violent action. Moreover, members of the dominant elite coalition can feel sufficiently assured of their privileges not to resort to preemptive violent strikes.

If power and privilege do not match each other, a natural state may violently transform itself into another natural state. In particular, more mature natural states that admit infinitely lived impersonal organizational forms can suppress violence among elites. Yet they may deteriorate into what is called in *VSO* a basic natural state with fewer independent organizational forms and even a fragile natural state which lacks almost all government-independent structures of mature natural states.

Once the state is invented, it becomes the "natural state of affairs." As *VSO* makes clear, historical evidence does not speak in favor of a natural tendency toward the more mature forms of natural states. The view of the ancients of a cyclical structure of political development going back and forth between natural states is partly supported by the evidence presented in *VSO*. Only open-access societies, though they may fail, do not systematically cycle.

Though *VSO* cannot explain how the anomaly of the great open-access society can arise and sustain itself, it makes it entirely clear that the private contract society is a political creation through and through. If it comes to the wealth of nations, it's politics—and not the economy—stupid! A timely reminder indeed!

Literature

North, D. C., Wallis, J. J., & Weingast, B. R. (2009). *Violence and social orders*. Cambridge: Cambridge University Press.

George Loewenstein Recommends "Self-Signaling and Diagnostic Utility in Everyday Decision Making" by Ronit Bodner and Drazen Prelec

George Loewenstein

》 *Bodner and Prelec assume that decisions generate two types of utility: the traditional economic utility associated with decision outcomes and a "diagnostic" utility that reflects the change in self-esteem produced by the decision.*

To the extent that other people lack information about us, we can sometimes signal our "type" via our behavior. For example, if a generous person would give to a beggar, but a selfish person would not, then one can signal one's generosity by giving. The fundamental psychological assumption behind *self-signaling* theory, attested to by the popularity of tests one can take to learn about oneself, as well as the myriad self-help books focused on self-discovery, is that people often lack information about themselves. Given such a lack of self-knowledge, we may make judgments about ourselves in the same way we do about others, inferring who we are from the actions we take. This creates a motive to take actions that signal desirable characteristics or traits.

G. Loewenstein (✉)
Department of Social and Decision Sciences, Carnegie Mellon University,
Pittsburgh, PA, USA
e-mail: gl20@andrew.cmu.edu

© Springer Nature Switzerland AG 2019
B. S. Frey, C. A. Schaltegger (eds.), *21st Century Economics*,
https://doi.org/10.1007/978-3-030-17740-9_31

Bodner and Prelec assume that decisions generate two types of utility: the traditional economic utility associated with decision outcomes and a "diagnostic" utility that reflects the change in self-esteem produced by the decision. These utilities are interconnected in that diagnostic utility requires a sacrifice in outcome utility: the greater the cost in foregone desired outcomes, the stronger the self-signal. They further distinguish between extrinsic and intrinsic self-signaling. Extrinsic self-signaling occurs when believing that one has a trait has beneficial effects for outcome utility. Believing that one is high in perseverance, for example, may aid one's ability to persevere and achieve extrinsic goals. Intrinsic signaling occurs when our actions are designed to directly improve diagnostic utility by leading us to believe that we have desired traits.

Bodner and Prelec's paper addresses a key question: How is self-signaling possible even if people know that they are doing it? For example, suppose one gives to charity to self-signal generosity. Shouldn't our knowledge that one is doing so for this reason undermine the signal value? Bodner and Prelec identify two polar opposite responses to this problem, while recognizing that the truth will typically lie between these extremes. With "face-value interpretations," people infer their own "revealed preferences" directly from their choices, ignoring the motive to self-signal which is partly responsible for these choices. In the charity example, this would mean simply inferring that one is generous from the fact that one gave to charity. At the opposite "true interpretations" extreme, people are aware of their desire for self-esteem and discount the value of the signal accordingly. Even in the latter situation, Bodner and Prelec show that self-signaling can enforce virtuous behavior, but it cannot eliminate all uncertainty about one's true character.

The theory of self-signaling has had a profound impact on economics. The concept of "moral wiggle room," for example, posits that people are often motivated more by the desire to appear generous (or to not appear selfish) than by genuine altruism. Research and theorizing on the role of incentives in prosocial behavior shows that rewarding people for virtuous behavior can, as a result of self-signaling (as well as conventional signaling to others), have perverse effects. Self-signaling also has implications for self-control, voting, perseverance, and many other topics of great importance to economics.

Literature

Bodner, R., & Prelec, D. (2003). Self-signaling and diagnostic utility in everyday decision making. Chapter 6. In I. Brocas & J. D. Carrillo (Eds.), *The psychology of economic decisions* (Vol. I, pp. 105–123). Oxford: Oxford University Press.

Ulrich Matter Recommends "Towards a Political Theory of the Firm" by Luigi Zingales

Ulrich Matter

>> *According to Confucius, the beginning of wisdom is to call things by their proper names. This holds for scientific endeavors in particular, as science tends to deal with names given to real things and not with the real things themselves (as famously remarked by Ockham).*

If economic terms are conceptually detached from the real things which they supposedly describe, theorizing based on these terms might be illusive. In spirit with Luigi Zingales, whose paper (Zingales 2017) I set out to discuss here, I conjecture that the term *firm*, as it is widely used in economics, is rather detached from the real thing it aims to describe.

As carefully laid out by Zingales, classical economic theory has used the term firm to describe atomic entities in free markets or simply equated the firm with a collection of contracts. Zingales contrasts this view with reality and draws two core conclusions. First, large shares of global economic activity take place within a few dozen firms (10 are among the 30 largest economic entities worldwide, when counting firms and governments). This means

U. Matter (✉)
SEPS-HSG/SIAW, University of St. Gallen, St. Gallen, Switzerland
e-mail: ulrich.matter@unisg.ch

© Springer Nature Switzerland AG 2019
B. S. Frey, C. A. Schaltegger (eds.), *21st Century Economics*,
https://doi.org/10.1007/978-3-030-17740-9_32

decision-making in vast parts of the global economy is neither under democratic control nor is it notably shaped by free markets as conceptualized in economic theory. Instead, a few individuals at the top of the largest corporations hold enormous economic and political power while being "hardly accountable to anybody." Second, he stresses that while this fact is largely ignored in economic theory, it poses the risk of a "Medici vicious circle," in which economic and political power reinforce each other, threatening both free markets and democracy. Zingales points to some key institutional factors which affect this risk and thus should be incorporated in a broader "political theory" of the firm: the conditions of the media market, the independence of the prosecutorial and judiciary power, and campaign financing laws. We can read this as a call for bringing the theory of the firm closer to political economics. I suggest two starting points for this agenda: (I) consider modeling media outlets as watching over governments as well as over corporations and (II) reconsider whether large citizen-based groups and corporations can both be modeled as the same type of special interest group.

Zingales' perspective also has policy relevance: If firms are small actors competing with each other in perfect markets, then it follows that whatever domain of a society is handled by firms is also shaped by market forces, and all that theoretically comes with market competition applies (the well-known theoretical implications for efficient factor allocation, consumer choice, etc.). Such a view is often implied in contemporary public discourse surrounding economic policy. Any call for privatization or deregulation implies—at least ostensibly—that decision-making ought to be shaped by market forces (as opposed to democratic/bureaucratic procedures, for better or worse). However, taking Zingales' arguments on board leads to a more cautious stance on this issue. The choice would then rather be whether decisions in a given economic domain should be made within one of two large hierarchical organizations: one controlled by democracy and in principle accountable to the public and the other controlled by ownership (democratic to the extent that shares are equally distributed among shareholders) but, as noted by Zingales, "hardly accountable to anybody."

Literature

Zingales, L. (2017). Towards a political theory of the firm. *Journal of Economic Perspectives, 31*(3), 113–130.

Peter Nijkamp Recommends "The False Duality of Work and Leisure" by Joy E. Beatty and William R. Torbert

Peter Nijkamp

» *The underlying proposition of this essay is that leisure contributes positively to the economy.*

Since the path-breaking work of Gary Becker, economists have frequently addressed the effect of leisure time on individual or collective economic outcomes (e.g. wages, productivity, efficiency, well-being). It has often been argued on both theoretical and empirical grounds that productive time and free time are enemies: more leisure time tends to reduce individual or aggregate economic performance.

In the past decades, serious scepticism has arisen on the dichotomy between productive time and leisure time. Both the new economics of happiness (Bruno Frey) and the premise of a positive effect of leisure time on economic efficiency have cast doubt on the trade-off nature of productive and free time. Leisure time and income are not necessarily antipoles: to achieve a higher position on the income ladder does not always require spending more hours on work and less hours on leisure. The idea that more leisure may prompt a lower income position clearly overlooks complementarity effects, especially

P. Nijkamp (✉)
Tinbergen Institute, Amsterdam, The Netherlands

Adam Mickiewicz University, Poznan, Poland

JADS, 's-Hertogenbosch, Hertogenbosch, The Netherlands

© Springer Nature Switzerland AG 2019
B. S. Frey, C. A. Schaltegger (eds.), *21st Century Economics*,
https://doi.org/10.1007/978-3-030-17740-9_33

over a longer time span: leisure activities may enhance individual creativity and skills.

The issue of leisure time in relation to other time has recently been put in an original perspective by Beatty and Torbert (2003) who postulate that, in general, leisure may have a positive influence on someone's personal development during adulthood as a result of intentional awareness-expanding inquiry from a certain age onward. Consequently, up to a certain limit, leisure is an intrinsically rewarding phenomenon, as it stimulates personal adaptiveness and hence increases the individuals' extrinsic economic value. Therefore, leisure time may have a positive impact on an individual's efficiency over a lifetime, and may prompt prosperity in the long run, so that people may also devote more time to discretionary consumption. Future economic expectations may thus positively be influenced by current leisure time. Clearly, the issue of time preferences is at stake here, in relation to the intertemporal elasticity of substitution between consumption.

Human capital is seen as one of the drivers of rising productivity, as it strengthens the quality of labour through a better use of knowledge, skills and health. But clearly, leisure can also positively impact human capital and hence labour productivity. Leisure can act as a productive factor that reinforces individual resilience and health outcomes, so that personal development and happiness are favoured by leisure time. Thus, leisure may positively contribute to labour externalities and hence to productivity results. This modern productivity-enhancing view of leisure of course does not imply that leisurely behaviour always leads to an economic optimum, but this trade-off is a matter of balance to be analysed through empirical evidence.

The new economics of leisure prompts a range of pertinent research questions, in particular:

- A proper definition of leisure time (e.g. in time dimensions, economic and noneconomic productive activities) and its variety in appearance
- Conditions under which complementarity between leisure and productive time emerges, at both individual (or group) level and at country (or comparative international) level
- Causal linkages between leisure time and economic outcome (e.g. income, innovativeness, happiness, psychological well-being, growth)
- Impacts of leisure on educational performance and skills and hence on quality of human capital
- Broader economic impacts of leisure time on leisure activity sectors (e.g. tourism, culture, nature)

- Microanalysis of the heterogeneity in leisure time use in relation to personal needs, self-esteem or quality of life
- Design of a fit-for-purpose production function with leisure and productive time as ingredients in a compensation model, complemented with the emerging leisure-time-oriented digital technology

Clearly, a new form of dolce far niente economics offers a better understanding of trade-offs and effects in a combined leisure-productive economy.

Literature

Beatty, J. E., & Torbert, W. R. (2003). The false duality of work and leisure. *Journal of Management Inquiry, 12*(3), 239–252.

Karl-Dieter Opp Recommends "Nudge: Improving Decisions About Health, Wealth, and Happiness" by Richard H. Thaler and Cass R. Sunstein

Karl-Dieter Opp

>> *Many of the factors of the extended economic model are not new to sociologists. But sociologists use these variables ad hoc. A major contribution of the Thaler/Sunstein book is to show how those variables can be integrated into a general theory of behavior.*

It might be strange that a sociologist such as the author of this essay contributes to a book on economic ideas "you should read and remember." I assume that the "you" in this expression refers to social scientists in general and, thus, to sociologists as well. The ideas I will focus on in this contribution are in my opinion so important that in particular sociologists should "read" them, "remember" them, and, most importantly, apply them in their explanatory efforts.

A major difference between economics and sociology is that sociology does not have at its disposal a general theory of human behavior that can be applied to explain a wide range of social phenomena. A minority of sociologists uses

K.-D. Opp (✉)
Prof. em., University of Leipzig, Leipzig, Germany

University of Washington, Seattle, WA, USA
e-mail: opp@sozio.uni-leipzig.de

© Springer Nature Switzerland AG 2019
B. S. Frey, C. A. Schaltegger (eds.), *21st Century Economics*,
https://doi.org/10.1007/978-3-030-17740-9_34

the economic model of man under the label "rational choice theory." The wide resistance against this model in sociology can largely be explained by the very restrictive conditions under which the model (or at least the best-known version of the model) holds. This model is aptly characterized in the book that this essay focuses on, namely, *Nudge* by Richard H. Thaler and Cass R. Sunstein (2008): the homo economicus "can think like Albert Einstein, store as much memory as IBM's Big Blue, and exercise the willpower of Mahatma Gandhi" (p. 6). One should add that homo economicus is also a pure egoist who has neither feelings for other people nor a bad conscience when he or she violates norms. The authors call these creatures *Econs*, whereas the real human beings of everyday life are called *Humans*.

One concern of the book is "libertarian paternalism"—ideas of how human behavior could and should be influenced. I focus on the other concern which seems most important to sociologists for explaining social phenomena. This is the idea that people "can be greatly influenced by small changes in context" (pp. 1–2). This implies that in principle all kinds of incentives can be explanatory variables. If in general small changes of the context are relevant, then all kinds of motives are to be considered, such as altruistic preferences, following norms, and punishing to impose pain on wrongdoers who fail to cooperate. The reason is that small environmental changes can only affect human behavior if they provide possibilities or constraints to achieve goals.

But Econs do not only differ from Humans in regard to preferences. Humans are fallible: they may choose rules of thumb (which may sometimes be wrong), they may adopt false beliefs, and they may act spontaneously without deliberating (see Part I of the book).

Advancing such a wide version of the economic model is not only a claim of the authors; the strength of the book is that its relevance is demonstrated with numerous convincing examples.

Many of the factors of the extended economic model are not new to sociologists. But sociologists use these variables ad hoc: in explaining a phenomenon such as protest, one has an inventory of factors (discontent, protest norms, number of others who protest, government repression) that are applied if one thinks this might yield correlations. A major contribution of the Thaler/Sunstein book is to show how those variables can be integrated into a general theory of behavior.

Literature

Thaler, R. H., & Sunstein, C. R. (2008). *Nudge. Improving decisions about health, wealth, and happiness*. New Haven, CT: Yale University Press.

Margit Osterloh Recommends "Do Women Shy Away from Competition? Do Men Compete Too Much?" by Muriel Niederle and Lise Vesterlund

Margit Osterloh

>> *Gender differences in preferences receive huge attention in the popular press. In economics this issue was neglected for a long time. Today, the situation has completely changed.*

To a great extent, this is due to Niederle and Vesterlund's article, which was the first to address whether women and men differ not only in cooperative and risk attitudes but in their attitudes to competition. A series of laboratory and field studies confirmed that there is a large gender gap between men and women of equal abilities in reaction toward competition. Women shy away from competition with men, and women underperform when competing against men.

In an experimental setting, the authors use the choice between pay for performance versus tournament-based compensation. They find that men chose tournament-based compensation schemes twice as often as women. The

M. Osterloh (✉)
University of Zurich, Zurich, Switzerland

University of Basel, Basel, Switzerland

CREMA—Center for Research in Economics, Management and Arts, Zurich, Switzerland
e-mail: margit.osterloh@business.uzh.ch

© Springer Nature Switzerland AG 2019
B. S. Frey, C. A. Schaltegger (eds.), *21st Century Economics*,
https://doi.org/10.1007/978-3-030-17740-9_35

results are obtained despite the fact that there were no differences in performance between men and women in the task to be fulfilled. These results are explained mainly by gender differences in overconfidence and in attitudes toward competition. There are two possible reasons: First, women are subject to a stereotype threat. The fear of conforming to a negative stereotype leads them to a lower willingness to compete. Second, being competitive against men causes identity costs of not conforming to a female role model, including a negative stigma of being bitchy.

These findings have shifted the discussion about the underrepresentation of women in top positions from the demand side—in particular discrimination of women by employers—to the supply side. If high-ability women opt out of competition with men, they cannot gain influential positions. This does not mean that women should be blamed for not throwing their hat into the ring. Rather, we should ask how to reduce stereotype threats and identity costs for women when competing with men. Niederle and Vesterlund have triggered a highly important debate about how to design institutions that help to reduce the gender gap.

First, the debate about affirmative action has been provided with fresh arguments: It has been demonstrated, that women—in particular high-performing ones—are more likely to enter competitions when it is announced that one winner is the highest performing woman. Such a "soft quota" induces women to outperform just other women instead of competing against a mixed gender group. Second, the gender gap in tournament entry has been shown to decline when individuals compete in teams. Third, a radical new idea arises how to limit competition, namely, that candidates could be randomly selected from a preselected short list. The rationale is that high-ability females are better motivated to apply for top jobs when they need not enter competition with men in the final round. Some examples in history imply that the (male) losers of such a selection process do not lose face and thus are more prone to cooperate with (female) winners. We plan to test this novel and unusual institutional design in a laboratory experiment.

Niederle and Vesterlund have inspired the debate about gender economics to a great extent. They have not only opened up a significant new research program but have encouraged new avenues to promote a higher representation of women in top positions.

Literature

Niederle, M., & Vesterlund, L. (2007). Do women shy away from competition? Do men compete too much? *Quarterly Journal of Economics, 122*(3), 1067–1101.

Martin Ravallion Recommends "Poverty Traps" by Samuel Bowles, Steven Durlauf, and Karla Hoff

Martin Ravallion

>> The idea of a poverty trap has been around for a long time but remains relevant today. In the classic model, over time, a low-level attractor pulls in any wealth-poor people nearby.

Yet, this coexists with other, preferred, equilibria—some stable, some not. Getting people out of the trap will not be possible with only a small transient gain in wealth, and people in their preferred equilibrium can be vulnerable to large downside shocks. The idea has important implications for development policy, including social protection.

The multiple equilibria can arise from the existence of threshold effects. The following are examples:

* Physiology: The fact that basal metabolic rate is positive means that the human body at rest requires a minimum food-energy intake before any physical work can be done.

M. Ravallion (✉)
Edmond D. Villani Professor of Economics, Department of Economics, Georgetown University, Washington, DC, USA
e-mail: mr1185@georgetown.edu

© Springer Nature Switzerland AG 2019
B. S. Frey, C. A. Schaltegger (eds.), *21st Century Economics*,
https://doi.org/10.1007/978-3-030-17740-9_36

- Lumpy "threshold goods": My students know that they have little hope of an earnings bump from just 1 day of schooling! There is some critical minimum for human capital.
- Punishment incentives do not bite when a person is close to the lowest possible utility. So a poor person may have a hard time convincing lenders (and others) that she is trustworthy. Thus, market failures can stem from poverty, as well as creating it.
- Economies can get caught in a poor-institutions trap—a PIT. This arises when institutional development is impossible at certain low levels of state capacity.

In another class of membership models, the persistence of poverty emerges from external effects of group membership. Sociologists have emphasized how the lack of role models can limit the life chances of children growing up in poor neighborhoods. The network effects get built into expectations about future prospects, inhibiting progress out of poverty.

Geographic externalities in economic development can have similar implications. In these models, living in a poor area makes it less likely one will escape poverty in the future, because the poor local infrastructure lowers the productivity of personal investments. This is a causal effect of location on poverty, not simply a geographic concentration of people with similar characteristics.

Another form of poverty trap can emerge with weak law enforcement and weak state capacities generally, such that poverty and corruption reinforce each other in a vicious cycle. People face a choice between legal and illegal entrepreneurship. Under certain conditions, one can find a "predation trap," a stable equilibrium in which predatory behavior is endemic and profits from productive enterprise are low.

Indeed, whole economies can be caught in a poverty trap. The combination of interdependence among households and/or firms with coordination failures has long been an argument for industrial policies and external development assistance. Coordination failures can also lead to recessions and even mass unemployment.

Once one thinks about it, poverty traps could well be pervasive. But they can also be hard to see. The signs of their presence could be just a relatively small number of destitute people. Or the trap may only be obvious in crises, such as famines, when institutions come under great stress. It is clearly hazardous to say from empirical observations at normal times that a trap does not exist. So please don't forget about this idea.

Literature

Bowles, S., Durlauf, S., & Hoff, K. (Eds.). (2006). *Poverty traps*. Princeton: Princeton University Press.

Susan Rose-Ackerman Recommends "Corruption, Norms, and Legal Enforcement: Evidence from Diplomatic Parking Tickets" by Raymond Fisman and Edward Miguel

Susan Rose-Ackerman

» *This paper illustrates an important strategy for empirical researchers to use when faced with difficult-to-study topics.*

It should inspire others to be similarly creative in locating usable data that can be an alternative to randomized controlled trials. Such trials, although a valuable tool, cannot answer many important social science issues. Even if done well, they ought not to replace other forms of data gathering.

Especially, if one wants to study illegal or immoral behavior, field experiments raise ethical concerns related to human subjects' research. An alternative, which has been used to good effect in the study of corruption and lawbreaking, is to find already existing data that allows one to delve into these difficult topics. Data from different sources can be triangulated to produce insights. Raymond Fisman and his co-authors have been at the vanguard of this research with papers on many topics, including stock market responses to the health crises of Suharto and Dick Cheney, and a study of Chinese bureaucrats' adjustments to benchmarks designed to reduce workplace deaths.

S. Rose-Ackerman (✉)
Henry R. Luce Professor of Law and Political Science, Yale University,
New Haven, CT, USA
e-mail: susan.rose-ackerman@yale.edu

© Springer Nature Switzerland AG 2019
B. S. Frey, C. A. Schaltegger (eds.), *21st Century Economics*,
https://doi.org/10.1007/978-3-030-17740-9_37

I have selected one example from his published work that uses data from the New York City Police Department on diplomatic parking tickets to study the cultural aspects of corruption and compliance with legal rules and to examine the role of incentives. Fisman and Miguel had the idea that UN diplomats might bring their attitudes toward compliance with the law with them into Manhattan. Thus, they studied the link between the incidence of diplomatic parking tickets and a country's score on the Corruption Perceptions Index published annually by Transparency International, an anticorruption NGO. In the early part of their time period, UN missions had no legal obligation to pay tickets. Nevertheless, they found a statistically significant correlation between the index and the number of tickets, corrected for the size of the mission. There was a temporary decline in offenses after 9/11, and a more permanent fall occurred when the US law changed to give UN missions a financial incentive to pay their tickets. The relative ranking of parking tickets still tracked the TI index, but the level fell. The paper both is suggestive of cross-country differences in respect for legal rules and shows that financial incentives affected the level, if not the relative position, of violations by country. True, the paper concentrates on a relatively minor offense and a group of elite offenders, but it suggests that although cultural differences cross borders, legal rules and financial incentives do matter.

Literature

Fisman, R., & Miguel, E. (2007). Corruption, norms, and legal enforcement: Evidence from diplomatic parking tickets. *Journal of Political Economy, 115*(6), 1020–1048.

Katja Rost Recommends "The Network Structure of Social Capital" by Ronald S. Burt

Katja Rost

>> *Burt is one of the first authors who connects sociology with economic insights and is widely received in both disciplines. In short, he argues that short-run advantages on the path to equilibrium in markets can be explained by network entrepreneurs: by brokerage in the social structure of relationships.*

For Burt, societies are markets in which people exchange a variety of goods and ideas in pursuit of their interests. Certain people and groups receive higher returns to their efforts by enjoying higher incomes, becoming prominent, or leading more important projects. From a human capital point of view, people who do better are more skilled. From a social capital point of view, people who do better are better connected. Social capital refers to features of social organization, such as trust, norms, and networks, that can improve the efficiency of society by facilitating coordinated action. Selecting the best exchange requires information on available goods, sellers, buyers, and prices. The structure of prior relations among people in a market can affect, or

K. Rost (✉)
Institute of Sociology, University of Zurich, Zurich, Switzerland
e-mail: rost@soziologie.uzh.ch

© Springer Nature Switzerland AG 2019
B. S. Frey, C. A. Schaltegger (eds.), *21st Century Economics*,
https://doi.org/10.1007/978-3-030-17740-9_38

replace, information. Such a replacement happens when market information is so ambiguous that people use network structure as the best available information.

A generic research finding in network analysis is that information circulates more within than between groups. Accordingly, prior research mostly relied on the closure argument as a network mechanism that facilitates coordinated action. Networks in which everyone is connected such that no one can escape the notice of others have been argued to reduce the risks associated with incomplete information. Burt counterargues that the network mechanism of brokerage opportunities may be more important for efficiency and coordination in markets. Holes in a social structure create a competitive advantage for a person whose relationships span the holes. The argument does not imply that people in two groups are unaware of one another. However, it means that the people are focused on their own activities such that they do not attend to the activities of people in the other group. Holes are buffers because people on either side of a structural hole circulate in different flows of information. Structural holes are thus an opportunity to broker the flow of information between people and to control the projects that bring together people from opposite sides of the hole.

The difference between brokerage and closure implies different roles for social capital in broader theories of markets and societies. Closure is about stasis, while brokerage is about change. The gains of brokerage disappear as more and more people build bridges across the same structural hole. Network entrepreneurs move the market to equilibrium by eliminating holes in the market where it was valuable to do so. So viewed, the social capital of structural holes is about a short-run advantage on the path to equilibrium. In some circumstances, the short-run advantage of brokerage can be a long-run advantage, for example, if the industry is subject to continuing change so that information continues to quickly grow out-of-date.

Literature

Burt, R. S. (2000). The network structure of social capital. *Research in Organizational Behavior, 22*, 345–423.

Christoph A. Schaltegger Recommends "Toward a Second-Generation Theory of Fiscal Federalism" by Wallace E. Oates

Christoph A. Schaltegger

❱❱ *In 1972, Wallace E. Oates pioneered an important branch of the economics literature, which flourished under the heading "fiscal federalism" and inspired many scholars in public economics. More than 30 years later, in "Toward a Second-Generation Theory of Fiscal Federalism," Oates nicely summarizes the findings of this literature.*

Oates distinguishes between a first and a second generation of theory on fiscal federalism. While the first draws more on welfare economics, the second points more strongly to political economy aspects and incentive problems. All research in this field began with the decentralization theorem. It refers to Samuelson's theory of public goods and shows that in a multilayered government, the assignment of tasks is efficient if organized in accordance with the principle of subsidiarity. The different levels of government should provide public goods according to their natural perimeter of effect. The aim of this institutional design is not only a perfect assignment of the public services at the different levels of the government, but this design also establishes the

C. A. Schaltegger (✉)
University of Lucerne, Lucerne, Switzerland
e-mail: Christoph.Schaltegger@unilu.ch

© Springer Nature Switzerland AG 2019
B. S. Frey, C. A. Schaltegger (eds.), *21st Century Economics*,
https://doi.org/10.1007/978-3-030-17740-9_39

corresponding taxing power according to the principle of fiscal equivalence. Since in reality a perfect assignment of public goods is not possible, fiscal equalization in the sense of an arrangement for fair cost sharing is of importance.

These early findings of the literature gave much room for interpretation. Later, the literature showed that decentralization is often advantageous even if spillovers exist and economies of scale are not exploited. First, decentralization strengthens the accountability of governments. Second, a sufficient large number of local authorities offer the possibility that citizens can vote "with their feet." Ultimately, this reduces the blackmailing potential of the individual state vis-à-vis the central government, while large regions are often considered "too big to fail."

The instability of federal systems was recently addressed. An important part comes from creeping centralization. Joint tasks between different levels of government and systems of revenue-sharing always give incentive to free ride on the fiscal commons. Thus, the overall challenge is to find appropriate institutions to make fiscal federalism self-enforcing.

We should read and remember Wallace E. Oates's work because it shows that:

- Fiscal federalism is an incentive device through which policy experiments and social innovation are possible. The process of trial and error generates real-world knowledge about pros and cons of policy choice.
- In order to reap the benefits of federalism, the principle of fiscal equivalence is crucial. Fiscal equalization as a system of mutually agreed grants is able to maintain fiscal equivalence if regional spillovers cannot be circumvented by the assignment of tasks.
- Joint tasks, revenue-sharing, and bailouts as elements of creeping centralization constitute soft budget constraints and give incentive to free ride on the fiscal commons. Insolvency rules strengthen federalism and foster hard budget constraints.
- A vital federalism needs a strong confederation and strong subfederal jurisdictions. The confederation must be strong enough to maintain market discipline in credit financing and by restricting the fiscal commons for the subfederal jurisdictions. The subfederal jurisdictions must be strong enough to live their autonomy, to experiment with policies, and to resist a centralization of their tasks and their power to tax.

Literature

Oates, W. E. (2005). Toward a second-generation theory of fiscal federalism. *International Tax and Public Finance, 12,* 349–373.

Mark Schelker Recommends "Salience and Taxation: Theory and Evidence" by Raj Chetty, Adam Looney, and Kory Kroft

Mark Schelker

>> *Recently, the integration of behavioral economics into public economics has made progress. The emerging field, behavioral public economics, is a fruitful combination of previously largely separate fields. A fascinating application focuses on the impact of the salience of a public policy on individual and social welfare.*

Salience refers to the degree of (in)attention individuals pay to an important aspect of a choice (e.g., a tax): even though individuals know about it and have experienced it before, they might not, or not fully, consider it when making the actual choice. As always, the basic idea of salience is also related to earlier concepts and, from that perspective, not entirely new. In public economics, for example, fiscal illusion is related to salience, but it is motivated from a different angle. Neglecting non-salient information can cause imperfect optimization. This is a significant extension of the traditional approach, in which the quality and quantity of information, or uncertainty, are key. An early and interesting study comes from Chetty et al. (2009). They ask whether

M. Schelker (✉)
Department of Economics, University of Fribourg, Fribourg, Switzerland
e-mail: mark.schelker@unifr.ch

© Springer Nature Switzerland AG 2019
B. S. Frey, C. A. Schaltegger (eds.), *21st Century Economics*,
https://doi.org/10.1007/978-3-030-17740-9_40

the salience of a value-added tax (VAT) affects individual decision-making. They analyze a setting in the USA, where the VAT is added only at the cashier, and show that individuals do not fully internalize it if only net-of-tax prices are displayed.

The study has all the merits of a paper published in one of the leading journals, but the breadth and depth of the study are still remarkable. Besides establishing the salience effect and contributing to the growing evidence of its existence, the authors go beyond the usual efforts to put their results into perspective. They generalize welfare analysis to include salience effects in their examination of tax incidence and deadweight losses and to derive policy implications. Naturally, the paper provided only a starting point, and further empirical evidence was, and still is, necessary to corroborate and extend the findings.

By now, the literature has evolved, and theoretical foundations to include salience effects in economics more generally have been formulated and applied in various fields. In public economics specifically, salience effects call into question some fundamental principles, such as tax neutrality. If the salience of a tax differs depending on whether the supply or the demand side is taxed, tax incidence changes, and liability side equivalence is violated. Besides distributional concerns, social welfare is also affected. A naïve interpretation could hold that low salience diminishes the behavioral response to taxes and reduces excess burden. However, low salience distorts individual optimization and causes welfare losses: individuals overconsume goods with non-salient taxes while still facing the same budget constraint. Such optimization errors might not only affect the consumption bundle but also individual consumption-saving decisions. When also considering political economy implications, the consequences could be even more profound. With self-interested policy makers, low tax salience is an attractive feature to maximize tax revenue and distort the incidence of a policy to benefit particular groups. If politicians actually have self-serving preferences for low-salience policies, the deadweight costs of public policy could be higher than expected. Consequently, salience may have important allocative and distributional repercussions and might affect other dimensions of public policy that go beyond taxation.

Literature

Chetty, R., Looney, A., & Kroft, K. (2009). Salience and taxation: Theory and evidence. *American Economic Review, 99*(4), 1145–1177.

Sascha L. Schmidt Recommends "Moneyball: The Art of Winning an Unfair Game" by Michael Lewis

Sascha L. Schmidt

>> *The efficient-market hypothesis states that asset prices fully reflect all the information that's extant, and therefore it is impossible to consistently "beat the market." Accordingly, market prices should only react to new information.*

Until the beginning of this century, professional baseball was seen as such an efficient business, because all teams should have been able to access the same established performance metrics of the players. Therefore, all players should have been priced properly according to the market, and baseball clubs thus could not systematically identify players who were over- or undervalued.

Examining the professional baseball market, the book *Moneyball: The Art of Winning an Unfair Game* tells the story of Billy Beane up until the year 2003. In 1997, he took over as General Manager of the Oakland A's, an averagely performing American baseball team with one of the lowest payrolls in Major League Baseball (MLB). In this bestseller, the author Michael Lewis explains how Beane made the Oakland A's successful through exploiting the systematic

S. L. Schmidt (✉)
Center for Sports and Management, WHU – Otto Beisheim School of
Management, Düsseldorf, Germany
e-mail: Sascha.Schmidt@whu.edu

© Springer Nature Switzerland AG 2019
B. S. Frey, C. A. Schaltegger (eds.), *21st Century Economics*,
https://doi.org/10.1007/978-3-030-17740-9_41

errors and inefficiencies in the then-existing market for baseball players. Due to Lewis's book, the term *moneyball* has become a synonym for data-driven decision-making that extends beyond sports. Other industries like professional services (e.g., law firms) have also applied the moneyball idea. In systematically taking advantage of information that other teams had, Billy Beane demonstrated that there are undervalued assets in a seemingly efficient market. Doing so, he was a visionary manager who revolutionized professional sports. From this perspective, moneyball can be seen as a valuable economic idea for the twenty-first century.

But how exactly did Beane turn around the fate of his franchise? He realized that he could apply contemporary economics to disprove traditional scouting methods, which were heavily reliant on subjective judgment and often compiled by former players and coaches. Instead, Beane used statistical data from the Society for American Baseball Research and focused on measuring in-game activity that correlated to winning games. Thus, Beane was able to identify the most relevant player statistics for team success and created new metrics to quantify the impact of a player on the result of a game. This innovative way of using data analytics allowed Beane to put together a very competitive baseball team at a fraction of the price paid by other teams. Under Beane's stewardship, Oakland emerged as the most efficient MLB team in terms of sportive success to payroll ratio since he became general manager.

The success of the moneyball idea inspired MLB teams across the league to implement database-dependent decision-making in their organizations, enabling less wealthy teams to compete against rich teams. The initial moneyball idea spread throughout the market, and this new information was subsequently included in market prices. As a result, the competitive advantage that the Oakland A's had hitherto enjoyed started to fade. From that time on, many other teams in the MLB have built upon the initial idea and further tailored moneyball approaches to their needs. The 2017 World Series was named "the first all-computer World Series" because both finalists, the Houston Astros and the Los Angeles Dodgers, were great believers and practitioners of data-driven analytics and scouting following the moneyball idea.

Literature

Lewis, M. (2003). *Moneyball: The art of winning an unfair game*. New York, NY: Norton.

Friedrich Schneider Recommends "Public Choice III" by Dennis C. Mueller

Friedrich Schneider

>> *Public choice is the study of behaviour at the intersection of economics and political science. An important branch of public choice, constitutional political economy provides important insights into the relationship between effective constitutions and the behaviour of ordinary political markets.*

According to Dennis C. Mueller (2003, p. 395), 'Public Choice can be defined as the economic study of nonmarket decision-making, or, simply the application of economics to political science. The basic behavioral postulate of public choice, as for economics, is that man is an egoistic, rational, utility maximizer'.

In the book *Public Choice III*, the following major areas are covered:

Why a state exists, voting rules, federalism, the theory of clubs, two-party and multiparty electoral systems, rent seeking, bureaucracy, interest groups, dictatorship, the size of government, voter participation, political business cycles, and contemporary political economy.

F. Schneider (✉)
Research Institute for Banking and Finance, Johannes Kepler University, Linz, Austria
e-mail: Friedrich.Schneider@jku.at

© Springer Nature Switzerland AG 2019
B. S. Frey, C. A. Schaltegger (eds.), *21st Century Economics*,
https://doi.org/10.1007/978-3-030-17740-9_42

113

Hence, public choice is the study of behaviour at the intersection of economics and political science. Since the 1940s, public choice has developed a rich literature, drawing from such related perspectives as history, philosophy, law and sociology, to analyse political decision-making (by citizen-voters, elected officials, bureaucratic administrators, lobbyists and other 'rational' actors) in social and economic context, with an emphasis on identifying differences between individual goals and collective outcomes. An important branch of public choice, constitutional political economy provides important insights into the relationship between effective constitutions and the behaviour of ordinary political markets.

Over the last 25 years, the use of the public choice analysis in politics and economics has overall not been as successful in policy advice and is not as important in overall economics as we, the public choice scholars, wish it to be. Hence, the victory of public choice in mainstream economics may not yet have arrived, and the share of public choice contributions remains small. Nevertheless, I am convinced that there will be a great future in public choice, as we face many political and economic problems (like should we have a European contribution, a debt brake, more federalism, etc.).

In addition, the European contribution to the future development of public choice may well consist in the introduction of new public-choice-orientated theories about the evolution of institutions and of new aspects of human behaviour. Especially the great variety of European economic and political institutions provides good opportunities to undertake this type of research for public choice scholars. In these fields, there are promising chances for a public choice perspective, and if young social science researchers take up these points, ideas in public choice will play a dominant role. Especially the latest development in Europe, which we can observe in many economic and/or political transformations, shows that there is a huge chance for public choice scholars to go into these areas, to be engaged in this type of research and to play a key role using the public choice analysis in the future.

To summarize, we should not forget the pioneering work of Dennis C. Mueller, *Public Choice III*, published in 2003. This book provides an excellent, intellectually challenging, and forward-looking tool in economics for this century.

Literature

Mueller, D. C. (2003). *Public choice III*. Cambridge: Cambridge University Press.

Ronnie Schöb Recommends "Economics and Identity" by George A. Akerlof and Rachel E. Kranton

Ronnie Schöb

People want to be happy, but happiness cannot be derived merely from economic prosperity. Economists, therefore, became more and more interested in other values that determine individuals' well-being and thus affect their behavior. By now, research on subjective well-being has identified many factors that make for a good life beyond economic prosperity. Social psychology, thereby, proved helpful in highlighting the great importance of social identity on subjective well-being. Individuals develop a "sense of self": a set of "self-images" that determines their identity. This personal identity depends on some purely individualistic "personal identity" and on a "social identity," which depends crucially on the way an individual is embedded in social groups. A shared "social identity" emerges based on cognitive criteria, such as shared fate, situations, and attributes, which can be either positive or negative. Belonging to a group is important for the individual's self-concept, as its norms, values, beliefs, and ideologies and one's adherence or nonadherence to them affect one's well-being.

George Akerlof and Rachel Kranton deserve credit for bringing these considerations to economic reasoning. They argue that identity strongly affects economic outcomes, and incorporating the concept of identity into an economic model of behavior thus allows a better understanding of many decisions that individuals make when interacting with others. For a variety of

R. Schöb (✉)
International Public Economics, Freie Universität Berlin, Berlin, Germany
e-mail: ronnie.schoeb@fu-berlin.de

© Springer Nature Switzerland AG 2019
B. S. Frey, C. A. Schaltegger (eds.), *21st Century Economics*,
https://doi.org/10.1007/978-3-030-17740-9_43

social and economic problems resulting from, for instance, interactions in the workplace or from social exclusion, they demonstrate how economic reasoning has to be altered when incorporating social identity. Identity, thereby, is not only a fixed determinant affecting well-being. Rather, it is in many circumstances a choice variable and choices of identity are among the most important economic decisions. Delimitation to this choice, for instance, in the case of involuntary unemployment, may act as a highly detrimental determinant of individual well-being.

For economic analysis, they divide the individual's total utility function into distinct individualistic and identity parts. The individualistic part represents the standard utility that depends on both one's own actions and the actions of others. It includes private consumption and leisure and depends on the provision of public goods and the consumption of goods by others that creates positive and negative externalities. The identity part of the utility function represents the utility derived from adhering to personally held objectives and beliefs and the ideals and social norms relevant to one's own social category. Identity is affected by one's own actions, but it is also shaped by the behavior, characteristics, and beliefs of others. This creates a new and important type of externality highly relevant for subjective well-being. Including identity when analyzing decision-making highlights that striving to behave according to the internal rules of one's social group is a personal choice, but altering self-identity by changing social groups may be an alternative choice. When taking these new types of externalities into account, the assessment of public policies may lead to substantially different conclusions than standard economic analysis suggests. Bringing identity to economics has opened up many promising avenues of research into what makes a good life and how politics might affect the determinants of well-being in different ways than we previously thought.

Literature

Akerlof, G. A., & Kranton, R. E. (2000). Economics and identity. *Quarterly Journal of Economics, 115*(3), 715–753.

Gerhard Schwarz Recommends "Why Capitalism?" by Allan H. Meltzer

Gerhard Schwarz

》 *The biggest advantage of capitalism for Meltzer is the fact that it is the only system which maximizes long-term growth and personal freedom at the same time.*

The book presented here brings neither an important theoretical breakthrough nor an original idea, but it gives a stimulating answer to a fundamental question, asked after the subprime crisis of 2008 even by many lukewarm supporters of the market economy. It is written by an outstanding economist, Allan H. Meltzer (1928–2017), who due to his modesty, seriousness, and unwillingness to produce headlines is less known and estimated than he deserves. The book is based mainly on American experience and written for the American public. However, given the importance of the US economy, it is, with its thoughtful arguments, inspiring for people all over the world. It refers to many economists, but even more important is its philosophical basis, above all Immanuel Kant. Meltzer writes on the welfare state and regulation, on fiscal policy, on progress, on foreign aid, and on inflation and often traces his arguments back to Kant and the enlightenment. The biggest advantage of

G. Schwarz (✉)
Progress Foundation, Zurich, Switzerland
e-mail: gerhard.schwarz@gerhard-schwarz.ch

© Springer Nature Switzerland AG 2019
B. S. Frey, C. A. Schaltegger (eds.), *21st Century Economics*,
https://doi.org/10.1007/978-3-030-17740-9_44

capitalism for Meltzer is the fact that it is the only system which maximizes long-term growth and personal freedom at the same time. But along with that go other advantages perhaps as important: the openness for change, the recognition of innovations, the adaptiveness to diverse cultures and situations, and the constant learning from mistakes.

On a more general level, the book develops three key messages. First, it argues against the widespread tendency in the developed world to consider the financial crisis as the end of capitalism. It has become fashionable also among technocratic, seemingly unideological economists to concentrate their work on the real and supposed deficiencies of the market economy and to forget the advantages and the fact that we know of no system that has produced better results. Meltzer reminds us that the only worlds seemingly better are the worlds offered by people who want to make their idea the general rule for everybody—and they are not real, but utopian.

Second, the book argues for realism. Meltzer makes clear that capitalism does not solve all problems efficiently, that there is room for collective action—though less than many believe. He also stresses the realism of capitalism, which treats "men and women as they are, not as in some utopian vision." Therefore, capitalism allows all kinds of behavior: besides all the positive behavior also self-serving decisions, dishonesty, greed, and venality. Meltzer does not deny this, but is convinced that capitalism induces honest behavior more often than other systems and that every attempt to follow one "right path" brings enforcement, often brutal enforcement. "The twentieth century is rife with promised ends that were never realized that turned into a justification for deplorable means."

Third, Meltzer shows persuasively that all moral criticism of capitalism confounds structural deficiencies and personal vices. Since capitalism is a human institution working with imperfect humans, it can only be an imperfect institution. Capitalism is, therefore, "not responsible for what goes wrong. People, most often people in powerful positions, are." But since capitalism disperses and limits power, while the alternatives concentrate power in a few hands, the moral damage of alternative systems is bigger. With this in mind, Meltzer expects capitalism to spread further—under one condition: that people continue to value both growth and freedom.

Literature

Meltzer, A. H. (2012). *Why capitalism?* Oxford: Oxford University Press.

David Stadelmann Recommends "Public Policy and the Initiative and Referendum: A Survey with Some New Evidence" by John G. Matsusaka

David Stadelmann

>> *In most developed economies, about half of gross domestic product is redistributed through means of collective decisions. The remainder is profoundly influenced by laws and regulation—by collective decisions again. Collective decisions themselves are more and more often taken by employing instruments of direct democracy.*

Citizen lawmaking is on the rise around the world. An increasingly critical, reflective, and educated citizenry requests more direct control over policy issues that are of importance to them. Modern communication technologies allow people to be better informed and to organize. Lamentations regarding shortcomings of pure representative democracy abound. The trend towards direct democracy is likely to continue throughout the twenty-first century.

Critics of direct democracy often argue that we know too little about its effects. This is not the case, and research on the effects of citizen participation in lawmaking is abundant. However, it is mostly limited to the United States and Switzerland, as these two countries have had extensive experience with

D. Stadelmann (✉)
University of Bayreuth, Bayreuth, Germany
e-mail: david.stadelmann@uni-bayreuth.de

© Springer Nature Switzerland AG 2019
B. S. Frey, C. A. Schaltegger (eds.), *21st Century Economics*,
https://doi.org/10.1007/978-3-030-17740-9_45

119

instruments of direct democracy for a comparatively long time. John Matsusaka provides an extensive survey of the literature on direct democracy. This makes his contribution an excellent starting point for researchers, policymakers, and citizens who wish to get an overview and contribute to improving collective decision-making in the future.

Of greater interest than a survey regarding the effects of direct democracy on public expenditures, revenues, debts, or specific electoral policies is the thought that policy needs to be evaluated in terms of responsiveness to citizen preferences. Of course, this idea, as most other ideas, has been advanced before in different forms, and it has been critically discussed in the past. Jean-Jacques Rousseau stated in the eighteenth century that all citizens could contribute personally or through their representatives to the formation of the general will, which is not necessarily the same as the will of the majority. Matsusaka, in line with a few other authors, revives this idea.

The thought that evaluations of the benefits of direct democracy, or any type of organization of collective decision-making, should go beyond the effects on fiscal policy or government structure is certainly worth remembering. If direct democracy improves collective decisions by making policy more responsive to citizens, public revenues and expenditure may increase or decrease, depending on citizen preferences. Moreover, the view that responsiveness is relevant suggests that direct democracy should not be seen as a substitute for representative democracy. Rather, it serves as a complement to it. Decisions through direct democracy will not necessarily become the standard way of all legislation, but if representatives neglect the will of the people, citizens themselves may act on failures in representation. Finally, focusing on responsiveness to citizen preferences highlights that direct democracy is not primarily a way of revealing the will of the majority. It represents a process in which citizens personally and together with their representatives and experts engage in an open, productive exchange of opinions, information, and arguments. This exchange facilitates the discovery of beneficial policies, and it permits the informed formation of preferences over policies.

Literature

Matsusaka, J. G. (2018). Public policy and the initiative and referendum: A survey with some new evidence. *Public Choice, 174*(1–2), 107–143. https://doi.org/10.1007/s11127-017-0486-0.

Bruno Staffelbach Recommends "The Lucifer Effect: Understanding How Good People Turn Evil" by Philip Zimbardo

Bruno Staffelbach

>> *What makes good people do bad things? What leads normal people to behave immorally?*

Such questions reside in ethics, law and politics, as well as within all people as moral subjects, as actors, as persons affected by decisions and as players in public and private organisations. There are two ways in which human behaviour can be explained. One looks for reasons in the character of the individual perpetrator. This has indeed become the rule in our ever more individualised world in the industrial west. The central questions are, Who is responsible? Who caused it? Who is to blame?

Philip Zimbardo, Emeritus Professor for Psychology at Stanford University, who became famous for his Stanford prison experiment, which in turn inspired the film *The Experiment*, chooses an alternative explanation. Zimbardo identifies the reasons in the situation, that is, in people's social context and its alternating expectations, norms and rules. The following questions are thus raised: Which conditions could have led to certain reactions? Which circumstances can play a role? What is the particular situation in which the participants find themselves?

B. Staffelbach (✉)
Faculty of Economics and Management, Center for Human Resource Management, University of Lucerne, Lucerne, Switzerland
e-mail: bruno.staffelbach@unilu.ch

© Springer Nature Switzerland AG 2019
B. S. Frey, C. A. Schaltegger (eds.), *21st Century Economics*,
https://doi.org/10.1007/978-3-030-17740-9_46

Following the Stanford prison experiment, Philip Zimbardo was able to identify the dynamics that can lead previously honest and law-abiding citizens to become criminals, ranging from the perpetration of economic crimes right through to organised genocide. What are the elements present within a situation that can lead to such acts? Philip Zimbardo identifies the following factors: conformity, compliance and allegiance, peer pressure and the need to belong, self-justification and rationalisation, situations where particular human qualities negate others and reduce people to numbers and also situations in which perpetrators hide behind powerful authorities, uniforms or chains of command or make themselves anonymous, thereby allowing their conscience, moral judgement and courage to slip away. Zimbardo's colleague from Stanford University, Albert Bandura, subsequently developed the theory of moral decoupling from some of these listed factors. This theory describes the process, whereby people are able to release themselves from their own moral programming by looking for good reasons for their own wrongdoings. For example, they might ignore the damaging consequences of their actions or reinterpret them or push the blame on to others; they might turn the victims into perpetrators or seek a new interpretation for their shameful acts by perceiving them as being in the name of a supposedly good cause.

If, however, it is the case that immoral conduct, offences and crimes are committed not only because the perpetrators are evil but because the 'power of the situation' triumphs over the 'power of the individual', as was demonstrated in Philip Zimbardo's prison experiment, then it follows that responsibility lies with those persons who, through their authority, through their resources or through their actions, acceptance or fundamentals created such a situation. Ethics in business is therefore not only a personal matter but rather a question for institutions, structures and processes. Leadership tasks would be significantly easier if moral questions could simply be excluded. However, this is only illusory. Organisations are not natural products. They have been created by people and are cultivated by people's vision of what is good, fair and reasonable.

Literature

Zimbardo, P. (2007). *The Lucifer effect: Understanding how good people turn evil.* New York: Random House.

Tobias Straumann Recommends "This Time Is Different: Eight Centuries of Financial Folly" by Carmen M. Reinhart and Kenneth S. Rogoff

Tobias Straumann

» The global financial crisis of 2008–2009 not only shook financial markets, world trade, and governments but also the economics profession.

It would be wrong to speak of a revolution, but a series of contributions by economists and economic historians have made it clear that we need to develop a deeper understanding of financial markets, debt dynamics, and macro-financial linkages in order to contain future financial crises. Of the many publications, one stands out: the book by Carmen M. Reinhart and Kenneth S. Rogoff.

The book is exceptional for several reasons. First and foremost, it has a title that has quickly become part of the basic vocabulary of bankers, economists, and policymakers. Whenever people talk about financial markets, sooner or later the phrase "this time is different" is thrown into the discussion. Better than any lengthy explanation, it encapsulates why financial crises keep returning. Obviously, we humans have a tendency to underestimate the potentially negative consequences of a financial boom because we overestimate our experience. We think that because we are aware of the dangers of a financial crisis,

T. Straumann (✉)
Department of Economics, University of Zurich, Zurich, Switzerland
e-mail: tobias.straumann@econ.uzh.ch

© Springer Nature Switzerland AG 2019
B. S. Frey, C. A. Schaltegger (eds.), *21st Century Economics*,
https://doi.org/10.1007/978-3-030-17740-9_47

we are immune to making mistakes. The opposite is true. Precisely because we believe ourselves to be well informed, we are particularly vulnerable to making wrong judgments during the boom period. Thus, the idea that bankers and investors suffer from huge losses during the crisis because they stop thinking during the buildup period is too simplistic. Some of them may be blind, but what makes the boom dangerous is that respected, intelligent experts and policymakers come up with sophisticated explanations why there is nothing to worry about, although the prices of financial assets are moving upward at an exceptionally rapid rate.

In addition to promoting this important conceptual framework, the book offers the first quantitative history of financial crises. Earlier authors studied individual episodes or clusters of financial crises, but they lacked the density and variety of data. By assembling an enormous series of graphs and tables, the authors succeed in documenting all different types of financial crises since medieval times for each country. Thanks to the data, Reinhart and Rogoff were able to predict that the recovery of the US economy from the recent mortgage crisis would last particularly long. They were also able to quantify the steep increase of fiscal deficits and government debt in the wake of the global financial crisis of 2008–2009. As their data are publicly available, we can expect many additional insights into the causes and causes of financial crises. Thanks to Reinhart and Rogoff, a new era in financial history research is in the making.

Finally, the book stands out for its simplicity and demonstrates that economic analysis can reach substantial conclusions without resorting to sophisticated models and econometric calculations. It opens a rich world of data and interpretations to a broader public and thus contributes to an informed public debate. It also reads like a plea for economic history. In a nutshell, the phrase "this time is different" is about how we interpret the past. At many departments, economics has become an ahistorical science. The book by Reinhart and Rogoff reminds us that this state of affairs has its price.

Literature

Reinhart, C. M., & Rogoff, K. S. (2009). *This time is different: Eight centuries of financial folly*. Princeton: Princeton University Press.

Alois Stutzer Recommends "Political Selection" by Timothy Besley

Alois Stutzer

>> *When a gulf opens up between citizens and politicians, as some diagnose for Western democracies these days, competitive elections are traditionally seen as a sanctioning mechanism that retrospective voters as principals use to tame their agents.*

In his contribution entitled "Political Selection," Tim Besley (2005) greatly complements this view with a rich set of considerations and ideas. He emphasizes that the delegation problem should also be addressed by focusing on selecting people into public office who are "competent and honest enough to discharge [their] duties" (p. 43). The paper is a magnificent specimen of scholarship in political economics. It offers an inspiring analysis on why it matters who gets into politics and on the trade-offs and mechanisms that affect political selection.

Selection is important as political decision-makers have discretionary power. Depending on their competence, they may react very differently to future challenges. As binding election promises are not feasible, the selection of people becomes decisive for whether they credibly represent and imple-

A. Stutzer (✉)
Faculty of Business and Economics, University of Basel, Basel, Switzerland
e-mail: alois.stutzer@unibas.ch

© Springer Nature Switzerland AG 2019
B. S. Frey, C. A. Schaltegger (eds.), *21st Century Economics*,
https://doi.org/10.1007/978-3-030-17740-9_48

ment a particular political position. Overall, political control over elected representatives is limited. In order to improve political decision-making, a careful selection of representatives is indispensable. In addition to their competence, honesty and public service motivation become crucial attributes of candidates.

This enriched view has several fruitful implications. First, the theoretical idea of a representative political agent without identity is replaced by a heterogeneous set of political decision-makers with different skills and motivations. Regarding the idea of good politicians, most people would agree that higher levels of competence and honesty are desirable. Second, elections sanction mainly indirectly, as voters see them as an opportunity to choose competent individuals who credibly represent their interests. If the electoral process partly allows the selection of good candidates, then the disciplining of bad politicians is implied. Third, a selection perspective emphasizes the pool of citizens willing to run for public office. Besley differentiates between four stages that affect the self-selection of good politicians: the attractiveness of holding office, the expected probability of electoral success, the outside options determining the opportunity costs, and finally his or her chances of reelection. Fourth, if coarse political behavior becomes the norm, more sensitive and consensus-oriented people are likely to decide not to run for political office, leading to a bad equilibrium of political selection. And fifth, institutions that are set up to hold politicians accountable or to reduce conflicts of interest firstly affect the selection into politics. For example, whether a position in public service is compatible with a political mandate is regulated rather differently across countries. Such institutional differences systematically influence the presence of former public servants in parliaments. But still little is known about how a federal structure or direct democracy is affecting political selection.

The paper teaches an important lesson to contemporary lamentation regarding elected politicians, namely, to study the underlying institutions that affect political selection: an idea to remember in twenty-first-century political economics.

Literature

Besley, T. (2005). Political selection. *Journal of Economic Perspectives, 19*(3), 43–60.

Cass R. Sunstein Recommends "Scarcity: Why Having Too Little Means So Much" by Sendhil Mullainathan and Eldar Shafir

Cass R. Sunstein

>> *It is common to think that economics is the study of scarcity – in terms of goods and services. But economists have rarely studied cognitive scarcity, at least not in any sustained way.*

A moment's reflection should be sufficient to show that human beings have limited mental bandwidth. That limitation has immense importance for our ability to focus and to act.

In a seminal book in 2013, Sendhil Mullainathan and Eldar Shafir opened up the whole topic of cognitive scarcity. Their basic claim is that if you are hungry, busy, poor, or lonely, you face the same difficulty: You are focused on a particular problem of scarcity, and that focus occupies your mind. Those who are hungry must think about how to get food, which means that they will not be able to think about much else. Poor people have to "tunnel" on the problem of making ends meet. In trying to solve immediate economic problems, they might enjoy a kind of "focus dividend"—no less than busy people, faced with a deadline, who sometimes accomplish great things in a short period of time. But tunneling and the focus dividend come with a "band-

C. R. Sunstein (✉)
Robert Walmsley University Professor, Harvard Law School, Cambridge, MA, USA
e-mail: csunstei@law.harvard.edu

© Springer Nature Switzerland AG 2019
B. S. Frey, C. A. Schaltegger (eds.), *21st Century Economics*,
https://doi.org/10.1007/978-3-030-17740-9_49

width tax," which means that poor people might not be able to attend to important matters that do not demand their immediate attention. They might not be able to solve health problems faced by their children; long-term planning will predictably suffer.

Mullainathan and Shafir support these claims with a wide assortment of empirical studies, including a demonstration that when poor people are initially asked to focus on an economic problem, they subsequently perform poorly on intelligence tests—even though they do fine on such tests when they are asked to take them without focusing first on a personal economic problem. Mullainathan and Shafir also show that hungry, busy, or lonely people are, in a sense, trapped by cognitive scarcity. If you are busy, you might not be in a good position to figure out how to provide yourself with temporal cushions, and if you are lonely, you are not likely to be in a good position to make friends. (Lonely people try too hard.) Poor people face the same problem; their limited bandwidth creates a poverty trap.

By drawing attention to the problem of scarcity, Mullainathan and Shafir make a defining theoretical contribution. It is connected to a growing body of work suggesting that if behavioral economics has a unifying theme, it lies in one idea: limited attention.

Their contribution is intensely practical as well. Too often, policies are designed with far too little attention to the bandwidth problem. New policies may come with paperwork or application requirements that undermine or defeat their own goals. In the context of poverty relief, for example, economic or educational benefits, or training programs, often impose paperwork burdens, which have the effect of reducing or discouraging applications, or of taxing time, which means that beneficiaries have less of that for more important endeavors.

Mullainathan and Shafir's work has important implications for countless issues, including some on which they do not focus. Think, for example, of people who are anxious or depressed, or in chronic pain, or in mourning, or in love. All these, and many more, are "tunneling," and they have limited bandwidth. That simple insight opens up a host of theoretical questions, many of which might be tested empirically; and it has implications for law and policy as well.

Literature

Mullainathan, S., & Shafir, E. (2013). *Scarcity: Why having too little means so much.* New York: Time Books, Henry Holt & Company LLC.

Guido Tabellini Recommends "A Model of Social Identity with an Application to Political Economy: Nation, Class, and Redistribution" by Moses Shayo

Guido Tabellini

In the standard approach to political economics and public choice, citizens vote according to their economic self-interest. They may have imperfect information and incorrect beliefs, but the driver of their political decisions is whether they expect to gain or lose economically from alternative political decisions. Sometimes, ideology is brought to bear on political preferences, but ideology is an exogenous black box that economists have not tried to explain.

This standard economic approach has been challenged by political scientists, based on extensive empirical and survey evidence. Sociology and psychology, much more than economics, hold promise to explain individual political preferences. But economists have been reluctant to abandon their traditional paradigm for lack of a precise and general alternative analytical framework.

Such an alternative has been suggested in an important paper by Moses Shayo, "A Model of Social Identity with an Application to Political Economy: Nation, Class and Redistribution", *American Political Science Review*, 2009. Adapting insights from social psychology and group theory, and following earlier ideas by Akerlof and Kranton on economic identities, Shayo argues that political preferences are shaped by social identities. Individuals identify with specific social groups, based on social proximity, and they adapt their political preferences to fit those of the group in question.

G. Tabellini (✉)
Intesa Sanpaolo Chair in Political Economics, Università L. Bocconi and IGIER, Milan, Italy
e-mail: guido.tabellini@unibocconi.it

© Springer Nature Switzerland AG 2019
B. S. Frey, C. A. Schaltegger (eds.), *21st Century Economics*,
https://doi.org/10.1007/978-3-030-17740-9_50

This line of thought opens up several key questions. First, what determines political identities? The main answer is similarity between the individual and the groups in features such as income, education, social status, ethnicity and labour market status. But the relative weight on these features is endogenous and can reflect their salience. Moreover, individuals can also identify with one group or another depending on how they are affected by economic policy—according to their economic interests. Finally, according to Shayo, the social status of the group also matters, as individuals seek to identify with groups enjoying higher status.

Second, what are the implications of social identification? According to Shayo, identification implies that the individual becomes altruistic towards the group. But other consequences could follow, in particular for political beliefs. For instance, individual beliefs about the effects of specific policies could become distorted towards the stereotypical beliefs of the group. Or individuals can be more easily persuaded by the positions taken by a group leader, such as a party leader. This reverses conventional wisdom about cause and effect: Trump did not win the support of Republican voters because he was able to exploit pre-existing and diffuse anti-immigrant sentiments; on the contrary, through his policy positions he created hostility against immigrants amongst individuals who had already chosen to support him for other reasons.

Third, how does political identification interact with policy choices? Because public policies change the salience of an issue, or the social status of a group, or they influence political beliefs, policy choice and social identities are jointly determined in equilibrium. This makes the analysis richer, but it also opens up the existence of multiple equilibria—a source of indeterminacy.

Exploring these issues, in theory and empirically, holds great promise and can bring about a revolution in the field of political economics and beyond.

Literature

Shayo, M. (2009). A model of social identity with an application to political economy: Nation, class and redistribution. *American Political Science Review, 96*, 57–73.

Mark Thoma Recommends "Learning and Expectations in Macroeconomics" by George Evans and Seppo Honkapohja

Mark Thoma

》 *Is it reasonable to assume expectations are formed rationally?*

In order to form rational expectations, people must know all of the equations describing the economy as well as the statistical properties of the shocks. In addition, they must use this knowledge to produce the best possible forecasts of how the economy will evolve over time. But how do people obtain the required information? Is it possible to use standard econometric methods to learn enough about the economy to produce rational expectations?

That question was answered in 2001 by George Evans and Seppo Honkapohja in *Learning and Expectations in Macroeconomics*. The essence of the adaptive learning (AL) approach described in their book is that expectations are not necessarily rational, at least not initially. Households, firms, and policymakers are modeled as econometricians, using least squares to update forecasts based on evolving data. Rational expectations (RE) are viewed as an outcome that would arise asymptotically as estimates converge over time, provided the RE equilibrium is stable under learning.

M. Thoma (✉)
Department of Economics, University of Oregon, Eugene, OR, USA
e-mail: mthoma@uoregon.edu

© Springer Nature Switzerland AG 2019   **131**
B. S. Frey, C. A. Schaltegger (eds.), *21st Century Economics*,
https://doi.org/10.1007/978-3-030-17740-9_51

The book presents the tools needed to determine whether or not a rational expectations equilibrium (REE) is stable under learning. These are known as E-stability conditions and they are often straightforward to compute.

In addition to the great number of methodological extensions since the 2001 book was published such as limited forecast horizons, the use of misspecified econometric models, heterogeneous expectations, and alternative forecasting rules such as trend-chasing behavior, there have been many important applications of AL models to specific topics. These include:

Equilibrium selection: When a model has multiple REE, as is generally the case in the macroeconomic models in use today, the E-stability principle can be used as a selection mechanism to identify which RE equilibria are stable under learning and which are not.

Bubbles and asset price dynamics: In AL models there is a possibility of recurrent deviations from the fundamentals price due to periodic bubbles and crashes. This can happen when agents use simple time-series econometric models to forecast returns and risk. Interestingly, a calibrated learning model can fit most features of US stock prices. AL has also been applied to exchange rates, the yield curve, and whether optimal monetary policy should lean against bubbles.

Monetary policy: In AL models, a stronger response to inflation is needed to keep expectations anchored to RE, and monetary policy has to be implemented carefully to ensure stability under learning.

Stagnation, the zero lower bound (ZLB), and fiscal stimulus: As is well known, in NK models, in addition to the targeted steady state, there is an unintended steady state with (mild) deflation at the ZLB. This situation has been examined under AL, and there is a "stagnation trap" region of low output and inflation expectations that pushes output and inflation lower over time. These dynamics can push the economy into a very low output steady state with below target inflation. Fiscal policy can be effective in avoiding or escaping the deflation trap if there are pessimistic expectations, e.g., arising from a financial crisis.

There are a wide variety of other applications as well, e.g., Ricardian equivalence does not necessarily hold in learning models, and Neo-Fisherian policy is completely at odds with the AL viewpoint, a testimony to the importance of the growing literature on adaptive learning.

Literature

Evans, G., & Honkapohja, S. (2001). *Learning and expectations in macroeconomics*. Princeton, NJ: Princeton University Press.

Benno Torgler Recommends "Economics Rules: The Rights and Wrongs of the Dismal Science" by Dani Rodrik

Benno Torgler

» *Economics, like any field, is subject to change, but change can lead to identity crises. What am I? An econ? A human? Perhaps even both? Schizophrenic, therefore?*

Does that mean I need to be nudged away from potential misbehaving? Is that approach fair? How did that happen? Did I (unintentionally or subconsciously) constrain my possibility set by forgetting other options? What about my neighbors, the Sociogs and Polscis, so close and yet so different? Are they living in warmer lands? Wishful thinking, who cares about geography in a post-economic era of Rio Grande. I feel like the search for the one and only universal model to map my twisted econ-human personality makes me even more depressed. What's the diagnosis? Physics envy, maybe?

Well, Dani Rodrik is a great state-of-the-art shrink offering a remedy with his 2015 book *Economics Rules: The Rights and Wrongs of the Dismal Science*, drumming common sense into my mind. Economics can be viewed as a collection of diverse contextual models that do not lead to a unique conclusion.

B. Torgler (✉)
QUT Business School, School of Economics and Finance, Queensland University of Technology, Brisbane, Australia
e-mail: benno.torgler@qut.edu.au

© Springer Nature Switzerland AG 2019
B. S. Frey, C. A. Schaltegger (eds.), *21st Century Economics*,
https://doi.org/10.1007/978-3-030-17740-9_52

A powerful panacea! Great to have an arsenal of models tailored to the context under exploration: "Knowledge accumulates in economics not vertically, with better models replacing worse ones, but horizontally, with newer models explaining aspects of social outcomes that were unaddressed earlier" (p. 67). Viewing scientific knowledge as a collection of cases helps us to relax and think of economic models as Rubinstein fables of interactions between humans. We may even become inspiring storytellers, able to cope with doubt and uncertainty. Fables do not need math per se, as shown so powerfully by Tom Schelling, a master of strategy-disciplined intuition. Even the use of math inspired by Samuelson's rigorous disposal of the rusty logical monstrosities of the past can become an esoteric animal in itself, as experienced by *Econometrica*, who had to pull the trigger on the axiomatic study of voting mechanisms, so detached from actual politics. Sure, Borges reminds us that we don't want perfection in the art of cartography; otherwise we end up with a conscionable but useless 1:1 real-world terrain map.

But beware of being contaminated by the Friedmanian malady that leads to confusion between unrealism and approximation. If Galileo neglects air resistance when studying the fall of bodies, fine, but I wouldn't trust a wingsuit manufacturer who tests its product ignoring air resistance as I try my first skydiving attempt in the Swiss Alps, at least, not if I hope to soar majestically through the air like a golden eagle. To enjoy the incredible scenery and more importantly avoid human fatality by biting the ground, I'm happy to be supported by a reality-connected Herb-Simonian safety system acknowledging that unrealism is no virtue. The skill of moving back and forth foxlike between candidate models and the real world is an art form in itself (It's hard and dangerous to be a hedgehog!). When faced with a compulsion to theorize, being reasonably world-savvy helps one stay out of trouble. Rodrik points to Einstein, who said "The whole of science is nothing but a refinement of everyday thinking," reminding us to be modest and humble: "At their best, economists' models provide some of that refinement—and not much more" (p. 81). "Much of what happens in the world of economics these days does reflect a more modest goal: the search for understanding one cause at a time. When ambition eclipses this aim, trouble often looms" (p. 145).

Literature

Rodrik, D. (2015). *Economics rules: The rights and wrongs of the dismal science*. New York, NY: W. W. Norton & Company.

Jean-Robert Tyran Recommends "Patience and the Wealth of Nations" by Thomas Dohmen, Benjamin Enke, Armin Falk, David Huffman, and Uwe Sunde

Jean-Robert Tyran

>> *Why do some countries grow rich while others remain stuck in poverty? This has been one of the most important questions in economics at least since Adam Smith published his Inquiry into the Causes and Nature of the Wealth of Nations in 1776.*

Standard economic theory explains economic growth with reference to the abundance of physical and human capital and technology. Empirically, these factors are indeed related to income and growth across countries and therefore explain the latter variables in a statistical sense. But this correlation does not reveal the deeper causes of capital accumulation. Many reasons have been suggested over the years, from climate to historical and institutional factors. Dohmen, Enke, Falk, Huffman, and Sunde ask whether having more patient people in a country makes that country richer. The idea is that more patient people invest more into human and physical capital and into productivity improvements.

J.-R. Tyran (✉)
Department of Economics, University of Vienna, Vienna, Austria
e-mail: jean-robert.tyran@univie.ac.at

© Springer Nature Switzerland AG 2019
B. S. Frey, C. A. Schaltegger (eds.), *21st Century Economics*,
https://doi.org/10.1007/978-3-030-17740-9_53

The authors collect data on representative samples of the population in 76 countries from around the world with a total of about 80,000 observations. They use an experimentally validated survey measure which essentially asks, would you prefer to receive an amount x today or a larger amount next year? The authors find a strong and robust relation between average patience, measured by the tendency to choose the later amount even if it is not much larger than the earlier, and the level and growth of income. For example, average patience explains about 40% of the between-country variation in income. The relation is robust to the inclusion of many other explanatory variables suggested in the literature and also holds at a regional level.

I think the paper merits to be included in the collection of economic ideas you should remember because it does not content itself with simply stating an idea (i.e., a hypothesis), but it also provides intriguing evidence in support of the hypothesis. Yet, a causal interpretation of the results is difficult. How does cross-country variation in patience arise in the first place? Might it be due to environmental or deep cultural factors? For example, Max Weber famously claimed that Protestant ethics is related to the "spirit of capitalism" and thus to capital accumulation. Interestingly, the authors find that their measure of patience is related to the share of protestants in a country, but Protestantism is by far not the sole explanation for the correlation.

The paper extends the economists' view of what types of capital matter and where capital is broadly speaking a factor that promotes production. The early economic literature only referred to physical capital and labor (which was later called human capital), while social capital has received attention as a potential driver of growth for only two or three decades. For example, Stephen Knack and Philip Keefer have shown (1997, in the *Quarterly Journal of Economics*) that countries with high levels of trust are more economically prosperous. The current paper provides evidence on the relevance of what could be called cultural capital, in the sense that places are richer where people are more patient.

Literature

Dohmen, T., Enke, B., Falk, A., Huffman, D., & Sunde, U. (2015, April 20). *Patience and the wealth of nations* (Working paper).

Ruut Veenhoven Recommends "The Broaden-and-Build Theory of Positive Emotions" by Barbara L. Fredrickson

Ruut Veenhoven

» *Happiness has long been a subject for philosophers but became established as a topic in the social sciences in the 1960s. Today two strands of happiness research have been developed: happiness economics and positive psychology.*

This paper highlights one of the ideas developed in positive psychology. Though the main focus of happiness research is on what makes people happy, a side issue is what happiness does to people, that is, what are the consequences of feeling happy or unhappy. A main contribution to answering this second question was made by psychologist Barbara Fredrickson in her seminal article, which I recommend.

R. Veenhoven (✉)
Erasmus Happiness Economics Research Organization (EHERO), Erasmus University Rotterdam, Rotterdam, Netherlands
e-mail: veenhoven@ese.eur.nl

© Springer Nature Switzerland AG 2019
B. S. Frey, C. A. Schaltegger (eds.), *21st Century Economics*,
https://doi.org/10.1007/978-3-030-17740-9_54

137

Tenets

The broaden-and-build theory holds that how well you feel affectively tends to *broaden* your behavioral repertoire, among other things, by fostering activity and widening perceptual scope. This makes you function more effectively, as a result of which you *build* more resources, such as economic, mental, and social capital.

Empirical Support

These benefits of feeling good appear in many cross-sectional studies, in longitudinal studies, and in experiments. Some examples of observed long-term effects of happiness are that (a) people who were most happy in their student years earn more in their adult life and (b) happy people live longer, even if their baseline health is controlled for. Likewise, experimental studies have shown that induced positive affect (c) enhances creative thinking, (d) fosters sociable behavior, and (e) protects against catching a cold. Probably because of this, happy people perform better at work.

Relevance for Happiness Economics

The conceptual focus of happiness economics is the subjective enjoyment of one's life as a whole, also called life satisfaction. This is not quite the same as positive affect; however, positive affect is a main component of life satisfaction, and there is much evidence that the broaden-and-build theory also applies to life satisfaction. As such, this theory gives substance to vague notions of reversed causality and calls for us to include consequences of happiness when model building and giving advice.

Implications for Economic Thought

Happiness is often seen as the end of a motivational process, economic agents deriving utility from consuming. The broaden-and-build theory shows that happiness is a factor in ongoing economic activity. In a similar vein, economists often assume that economic behavior is driven by unhappiness, whereas the broaden-and-build theory shows that positive enjoyment of life helps us function well.

A wider relevance of the broaden-and-build theory is that it marks the importance of affective experience, while the focus in economic thought is on cognitive calculation. The ability to feel good or bad is part of an intuitive orientation system, which we share with other higher animals. Feeling good typically reflects that our needs are being gratified. Needs should not be equated with wants. Needs are unconscious and reflect, at best, in affective experience; wants are mental constructs you are aware of. Wants do not always fit needs, and wants may be endless, while needs are not. In this view, maximizing utility requires a focus on need gratification and hence measurement of happiness.

Literature

Fredrickson, B. L. (2004). The broaden-and-build theory of positive emotions. *Philosophical Transactions, Biological Sciences, 359,* 1367–1377.

Carl Christian von Weizsäcker
Recommends "Trills Instead of T-Bills: It's Time to Replace Part of Government Debt with Shares in GDP" by Mark J. Kamstra and Robert J. Shiller

Carl Christian von Weizsäcker

>> *Kamstra and Shiller propose a financial instrument issued by the government which they call "Trills."*

A unit Trill is the right to receive from the government an annual payment equal to 1 trillionth of the country's GDP in nominal terms. Thus, a US Trill would pay $ 19.39 for the year 2017, because the US GDP in 2017 was 19,390.60 billion US dollars. We may surmise that the market value of a unit of such security is somewhere between $ 500 and $ 2000.

Kamstra and Shiller argue that this Trill security would fill a gap in the world of securities. "Standard mean-variance (return versus risk) optimization over asset classes, including the estimated return to holding Trills, suggests that Trills might allow investors a return very nearly as high as the S&P 500, with half the volatility. Indeed, investors gain a much higher return and lower volatility than if Trills are excluded from the mix. This mean variance optimization produces an optimal portfolio composition of 28% of assets in long-term bonds, 38% in the S&P 500 index and 34% in Trills. Thus, the addition

C. C. von Weizsäcker (✉)
Max Planck Institute for Research on Collective Goods, Bonn, Germany
e-mail: weizsaecker@coll.mpg.de

© Springer Nature Switzerland AG 2019
B. S. Frey, C. A. Schaltegger (eds.), *21st Century Economics*,
https://doi.org/10.1007/978-3-030-17740-9_55

141

of Trills to the asset mix available today would likely have a dramatic impact on investor portfolio composition and investor well-being" (pp. 3–4).

Kamstra and Shiller also discuss the fiscal benefit arising from such Trills. Indeed, payments by the government for the Trill form of debt service are procyclical, and thus they vary in parallel with government tax receipts. This eases the debt burden of the government's automatic stabilizer and provides additional leeway for countercyclical fiscal policy.

As I have argued (*German Economic Review* 2014), we live in a twenty-first-century world with a negative natural rate of interest: if it were not for the substantial public debt, the full employment real rate of interest would be strongly negative. At a nonnegative risk-free real rate of interest, private savings substantially exceed private investments. If the world wants to maintain price stability and full employment, public debt is the outlet needed for coping with the excess of private savings over private investment. For the OECD-plus-China area, using a wide definition of public debt, it is my estimate that at least one third of private wealth is held in the form of public debt—and less than half of private wealth is held in the form of real capital (excluding land).

Moreover, the economic and demographic forces causing the gap between private savings and private investment have an upward trend. Thus, the public debt required to maintain a nonnegative risk-free real rate of interest is likely to grow further. It is quite possible that it reaches a share of private wealth of 50% at some time before the year 2100.

The stability of the system then depends on a substantial share of public debt to be held in the form of equity like Trills.

We should note that many social security systems already have some similarity with Trills. In Germany, it is the average current wage of presently active employees which plays a role in actual pensions similar to the current GDP in the case of Trills. Thus, instruments similar to Trills are already here. Given the popularity of the social security system, we can predict that Trills will be tremendously popular.

Literature

Kamstra, M. J. & Shiller, R. J., (2010, September). Trills instead of T-Bills: It's time to replace part of government debt with shares in GDP. *The Economists' Voice*, www.bepress.com/ev

Gert G. Wagner Recommends "Homo Ignorans: Deliberately Choosing Not to Know" by Ralph Hertwig and Christoph Engel

Gert G. Wagner

>> *For decades, economics ignored psychological traits and mechanisms. Cognitive psychology offers economists more than just "nudging." It also offers "boosting," which helps people get closer to the rational agents populating economic models. But psychology also deals with deliberately choosing not to know, introducing the Homo Ignorans.*

For decades, economics ignored psychological traits and mechanisms. It did not generally negate the importance of tastes and the heterogeneity of agents, but economic models omitted explicitly psychological variables (one exception being the "law" of diminishing marginal utility, which was not analyzed in detail but taken as a fixed assumption). In the meantime, the increased prevalence of surveys collecting not only economic and social variables but also psychological constructs (for instance, the German Socio-Economic Panel Study (SOEP)) leads to a growing interest in psychological traits among empirical economists. Thus, developmental and personal psychological con-

G. G. Wagner (✉)
DIW, Berlin, Germany
e-mail: gwagner@diw.de

© Springer Nature Switzerland AG 2019
B. S. Frey, C. A. Schaltegger (eds.), *21st Century Economics*,
https://doi.org/10.1007/978-3-030-17740-9_56

cepts are now incorporated in, for example, labor economics. However, other important dimensions of psychological science remain largely ignored by economists. This is especially true with regard to the psychology of cognition—long after Daniel Kahneman, a psychologist studying human decision-making, won the Nobel Prize in Economics.

Cognitive psychology offers economists more than just "nudging," popularized by economist Richard Thaler, winner of the 2017 Nobel Prize in Economics. It also offers "boosting," which stresses the possibility to foster extant competencies, thus enabling people to exercise their own agency. Boosts can target risk literacy (e.g., by offering transparent information) and decision-making competences (e.g., by suggesting smart and simple rules of thumb). Importantly, boosting helps people get closer to the rational agents populating economic models. However, boosting mechanisms are very different from the complex calculations that economic models rely on. Boosts are often simple processes, such as decision trees.

Here, I recommend a psychological article addressing a subject matter that strongly counters the notion of economists that more information is always better. It deals with *Deliberately Choosing Not to Know*, introducing the *Homo Ignorans*.

Psychologist Ralph Hertwig and legal scholar Christoph Engel start with the observation that people often choose not to know. For example, many people do not want to know if their individual-specific genetic endowment increases their risks for serious diseases. The authors examples include Nobel laureate James Watson, who chose not to know his own genetic status for late-onset Alzheimer's disease.

More importantly, choosing to be *Homo Ignorans* may be a strategic tool to evade moral responsibility, for example, in the context of unfair trade.

Deliberate ignorance is also a vital part of society. For example, as nobody chooses their own sex at birth, social systems are designed to operate under a veil of ignorance, ensuring that the rights and duties within the system do not, at least ideally, hinge on immutable characteristics.

Ignorance can be efficient (a concept loved by economists). Consider one-stop shoppers who visit only Amazon and no other supplier. It saves time and makes sense if you trust Amazon (but trust is not loved by economists). This is an example of deliberate ignorance, and as the digital economy continues to grow, with its massive amounts of information, *Homo Ignorans* might be a wise man more than ever.

Whether ignorance is bliss or not depends on the circumstances. An example of harmful ignorance is the behavior of professional economists who ignore the psychological literature (at least they do not cite it).

Literature

Hertwig, R., & Engel, C. (2016). Homo ignorans: Deliberately choosing not to know. *Perspectives on Psychological Science, 11*(3), 359–372.

Hannelore Weck-Hannemann Recommends "Orchestrating Impartiality: The Impact of 'Blind' Auditions on Female Musicians" by Claudia Goldin and Cecilia Rouse

Hannelore Weck-Hannemann

>> *Discrimination is a hot topic—and so it will be in the twenty-first century.*

Seminal contributions in economics have focused on disparities in earnings between groups, including gender differences. The widely used gap method attempts to control all relevant determinants of wage differentials, with the remaining gap undefined. The unobservable is subsequently interpreted as discrimination.

In fact, it is extremely difficult to measure discrimination directly. But two resourceful researchers (Goldin and Rouse 2000) have discovered an innovative approach to directly investigate and prove discrimination. They were successful in the field of culture by interpreting and evaluating the changes in the selection process for musicians in symphony orchestras in the USA as a field experiment.

In an attempt to overcome gender-biased hiring, a number of orchestras have revised their recruitment procedures in temporal and procedural order. Some orchestras opened the hiring process to a broader range of candidates,

H. Weck-Hannemann (✉)
Department of Public Finance, University of Innsbruck, Innsbruck, Austria
e-mail: Hannelore.Weck@uibk.ac.at

© Springer Nature Switzerland AG 2019   **147**
B. S. Frey, C. A. Schaltegger (eds.), *21st Century Economics*,
https://doi.org/10.1007/978-3-030-17740-9_57

and others adopted 'blind' auditions, in which screens conceal the identity and gender of applicants from the jury.

This variation of the audition process, including the introduction of screens at different times, allows us to assess their use as treatment. In an individual fixed-effects framework, it is possible to analyze whether sex is considered in the hiring process. The use of blind auditions should make the procedure more impartial, which should affect the employment of women.

The findings are remarkable: blind auditions significantly reduce gender-biased hiring and increase the number of female musicians in symphony orchestras. Using a screen increases the likelihood that a female musician will advance to the next round of the application procedure by 11 percentage points. In the audition sample used, the switch to blind auctions explains about 1/3 of the increase in the proportion of females among new hires, and another 1/3 is the result of an increased pool of female candidates. According to analysis using roster data, blind auditions account for 25% of the increase in the percentage of orchestra musicians who are female.

The publication has received much attention—although the study contains some caveats to which the authors have already referred: not only that some of the estimates have large standard errors and there is one persistent effect in the opposite direction. In addition, the data used are confidential and there-fore may not be made available to other researchers. But all the more impressive is the high level of attention and positive feedback that the study design and results have received.

The significance of the study also goes far beyond the concrete application in the field of culture and women's discrimination. The analysis suggests that a curtain helps not only in the fight against gender discrimination but also in other forms of discrimination such as age, race, religion, nationality, and so on. The question is rather how blindness and ignorance in the application process can be transferred to other situations and constellations. It is thanks to the authors that they have stimulated further considerations with their work.

Literature

Goldin, C., & Rouse, C. (2000). Orchestrating impartiality: The impact of 'blind' auditions on female musicians. *The American Economic Review, 90*(4), 715–741.

Barry R. Weingast Recommends "Economic Backwardness in Political Perspective" by Daron Acemoglu and James A. Robinson

Barry R. Weingast

» *Why do so many governments in developing countries pursue political impediments to economic development? In particular, why do they fail to provide secure property rights, enforce contracts, and, generally, reform policies hindering markets?*

This paper is one of my favorites in the extensive and powerful Acemoglu and Robinson et al. corpus. Although it is not among their most recognized works, it deserves greater attention. This paper demonstrates the power of the political economics approach, especially how political institutions directly influence economic development.

Acemoglu and Robinson ask, why do so many governments in developing countries pursue political impediments to economic development? In particular, why do they fail to provide secure property rights, enforce contracts, and, generally, reform policies hindering markets?

B. R. Weingast (✉)
Hoover Institution, Stanford University, Stanford, CA, USA

Department of Political Science, Stanford University, Stanford, CA, USA
e-mail: weingast@stanford.edu

© Springer Nature Switzerland AG 2019
B. S. Frey, C. A. Schaltegger (eds.), *21st Century Economics*,
https://doi.org/10.1007/978-3-030-17740-9_58

Acemoglu and Robinson answer that policies supporting the growth of markets create new interests and wealth, which can be marshaled against incumbent political officials, either through elections or through violence. Rationally fearing replacement, political incumbents are often unwilling to pursue policies and institutions that generate widespread growth and wealth. Acemoglu and Robinson show that such blocking is more likely to arise when political stakes are higher and in the absence of external threats. These scholars argue that their model explains why Britain, Germany, and the United States industrialized during the nineteenth century, while the monarchy and the landed aristocracy in Russia and Austria-Hungary blocked development.

At the risk of vastly over-simplifying, consider a poor, underdeveloped country with a ruling elite and a pro-democratic opposition. As the incumbent politicians, the elite are at risk for being replaced by the opposition. Policy choice by the elite affects the probability the incumbents retain power. The elite face the choice between retaining the status quo and market-enhancing polices that increase total economic surplus.

If the elite choose market-enhancing policies, then the probability that the opposition replace the incumbent elite is p_H. If the elite chose to do nothing, then the probability the opposition replaces the elite is p_L, where $0 \leq p_L \leq p_H \leq 1$. If the opposition replaces the elite, it must decide proportion of the social surplus, s ($0 \leq s \leq 1$), to share with the elite. Finally, we assume that the value of market-enhancing policies is worth $A > 1$. Economic efficiency (maximizing the surplus) requires the choice of market-enhancing policies.

The elite thus face a trade-off. Choosing market-enhancing policies raises the total surplus but lowers the probability the elite retain power. Unless the efficiency gains are really large, the elite will suppress market-enhancing policies and maintain the status quo (technically, the elite will choose market-enhancing policies when $A > (1 - p_L)/(1 - p_H)$).

The problem is one of political commitment. If the opposition had the ability to pre-commit itself to sharing a sufficient portion of the increased surplus with the elite, then the elite would choose market-enhancing policies and institutions. But most poor developing countries lack to institutional mechanisms to make any promise by opposition credible. Pareto-improving bargains fail to occur because they lack credibility.

This paper is among the best in the literature on the political economics of development at illustrating why politics and political institutions matter for economic development and why some configurations of political institutions impede the development process. In the absence of commitment mechanisms, developing countries remain undeveloped due to the divergence of interests between the incumbent government and the larger citizenry.

This short summary of AR's backwardness game is necessarily overly simplified, but it can be made more interesting by considering a range of comparative statics.

Literature

Acemoglu, D., & Robinson, J. A. (2006). Economic backwardness in political perspective. *American Political Science Review, 100*, 115–131.

Barbara E. Weissenberger Recommends "Management Control Systems: Performance Measurement, Evaluation, and Incentives" by Kenneth A. Merchant and Wim A. Van der Stede

Barbara E. Weissenberger

>> *Understanding behavioral deviations in firms is usually not possible through focusing on single control instruments or one grand theory. Instead, a holistic approach is needed.*

A key challenge in management is to achieve behavioral control, i.e., to ensure employees contribute effectively to a firm's goals. To this end, a broad array of instruments has been developed in modern business administration. These instruments comprise, amongst others, techniques to break strategies down into action plans, create organizational structures, select and train employees, provide budgets and elaborate incentive schemes, monitor results, and analyze and solve technical business problems.

Nonetheless, anecdotal evidence and systematic empirical research yield but mixed results. We still observe undesired behaviors, from major scandals, like banks manipulating the LIBOR interest rate, the Diesel emission scandal in the automotive industry, or the misuse of user data by Internet firms, to

B. E. Weissenberger (✉)
Management Control and Accounting, Heinrich Heine University, Duesseldorf, Germany

Accounting, Bucerius Law School, Hamburg, Germany
e-mail: Barbara.Weissenberger@hhu.de

© Springer Nature Switzerland AG 2019
B. S. Frey, C. A. Schaltegger (eds.), *21st Century Economics*,
https://doi.org/10.1007/978-3-030-17740-9_59

small-scale misconduct that does not make a news item, such as petty theft, information manipulation, budget gaming, and resource waste through negligent decision-making.

Over the last decades, researchers have learned (somewhat painfully) that understanding behavioral deviations in firms is usually not possible through focusing on single control instruments or one grand theory. Instead, a holistic approach is needed. It was Kenneth A. Merchant and Wim A. Van der Stede who in 2003 introduced their seminal economic object-of-control framework, thus allowing integration of the multifaceted theoretical lenses from psychology, sociology, politics, economics, or philosophy for understanding, analyzing, and even resolving management control problems.

In a nutshell, Merchant's and Van der Stede's idea is brilliantly clear-cut. First, management control problems regarding a firm's given strategy are identified: Is the desired employee behavior also the most likely one? If not, any reason for behavioral deviations is then decomposed into three roots:

- Employees may not understand what is expected of them (lack of direction),
- They may not want to act upon these expectations (lack of motivation), and/or
- They may not have the necessary resources or capabilities, or the task in itself is insoluble (personal limitations).

If a management control problem cannot feasibly be avoided by task automation, elimination, or centralization, Merchant's and Van der Stede's framework proposes addressing it by means of a carefully designed management control package, combining:

- Results controls, such as pay-for-performance systems,
- Action controls, such as physical constraints, preaction reviews, and action accountability, and/or
- People controls comprising personnel controls, such as selection, training, placement or job design, as well as cultural controls, such as codes of conduct, group rewards, and tone at the top.

In a well-designed management control package, all controls are chosen in combination, so as to interact with each other, reinforcing their impact as well as offsetting respective risks and side effects.

Besides its appealingly simple structure giving credit to the Occam's razor principle, the object-of-control framework provides a general structure to address management control problems with multiple embedded issues and incomplete or unstructured information. At the same time, it is flexible enough to apply in changing corporate environments if new controls emerge, for instance, through the rise of digital technologies or through an increased need for social and ecological responsible behavior. It is therefore an economic idea well worth remembering in 21st century economics and business research as well as practice.

Literature

Merchant, K. A., & Van der Stede, W. A. (2017). *Management control systems. Performance measurement, evaluation, and incentives* (4th ed.). Harlow: Pearson First published in 2003. ISBN: 978-1-292-11055-4.

Ludger Woessmann Recommends "Measuring the Impacts of Teachers II: Teacher Value-Added and Student Outcomes in Adulthood" by Raj Chetty, John N. Friedman, and Jonah E. Rockoff

Ludger Woessmann

>> *Increasing evidence shows that the long-term prosperity of individuals and societies alike depends crucially on their education and skills. This makes a better understanding of the determinants of educational achievement a pressing question for research and policy.*

The fascinating research by Chetty, Friedman, and Rockoff shows that high-quality teachers—those whose students show higher learning gains—have very strong effects on their students' lifetime outcomes. Their results suggest that if you replaced a teacher in the bottom 5% of the distribution with just an average teacher, this would raise the discounted value of the total lifetime income of the students in the classroom by roughly a quarter of a million dollars.

Apart from the main idea that the quality of teachers is crucial for children's future well-being, I would like to emphasize three specific ideas that make this

L. Woessmann (✉)
Department of Economics, University of Munich, Munich, Germany

ifo Center for the Economics of Education, Munich, Germany
e-mail: woessmann@ifo.de

© Springer Nature Switzerland AG 2019
B. S. Frey, C. A. Schaltegger (eds.), *21st Century Economics*,
https://doi.org/10.1007/978-3-030-17740-9_60

research so great: measuring teacher quality by their value added to test scores, using big data to answer important research questions, and using econometric methods for causal identification.

First, teacher quality is measured by their "value-added," defined as the average test-score gain they produce in their students, adjusted for differences in student characteristics including their previous scores. In the first part of their research, the authors show that teacher value-added is a good measure of teacher quality in the sense that value-added measures provide unbiased estimates of teachers' causal impacts on student achievement. For example, when a high value-added teacher enters a school, test scores in the respective grade rise immediately.

Second, to test whether teacher value-added really has an effect on students' long-term outcomes, you need data that only a decade ago most of us thought would be impossible to have. But Chetty, Friedman, and Rockoff managed to get permission to link school district records to tax records at the individual level for roughly 1 million children. That is, they estimate the value-added of teachers in grades 3–8 in New York City covering 20 years of student test scores. And then, using US tax records, they link these teacher quality measures to the students' actual later outcomes in early adulthood such as earnings, college attendance, and teenage births.

Third, their basic estimation of the long-term impact of teacher quality relates teachers' value-added measures to their students' outcomes in adulthood. This cross-sectional comparison requires the assumption that, conditional on the rich set of observed controls including students' prior test scores and demographic characteristics, there are no unobserved determinants of adult outcomes that are related to teachers' value-added. This approach is validated in a clever quasi-experimental design that exploits variation from teacher turnover: changes in average teacher quality between consecutive cohorts in the same school that emerge from high-quality teachers of a specific grade leaving the school between the two cohorts.

The results show that students assigned to high value-added teachers are more likely to go to college, earn higher incomes, and are less likely to be teenage mothers. Great teachers create great value, and test-score-based value-added measures are one useful way of identifying such teachers. Countries that want to improve the future well-being of their citizens should focus on attracting, developing, and retaining a high-quality teaching force.

Literature

Chetty, R., Friedman, J. N., & Rockoff, J. E. (2014). Measuring the impacts of teachers II: Teacher value-added and student outcomes in adulthood. *American Economic Review, 104*(9), 2633–2679.

Klaus F. Zimmermann Recommends "Identity Economics: How Our Identities Shape Our Work, Wages, and Well-Being" by George A. Akerlof and Rachel E. Kranton

Klaus F. Zimmermann

>> *Economists are used to explaining individual behavior by market prices, total income, and preferences through a utility evaluation of alternative actions.*

A new research agenda adds an identity variable that depends on the individual's actions, its assigned social categories, and the actions of others. Choices are then based on both monetary incentives and identity issues. This way, social norms related to expected behavior in social groups can influence individual behavior and choices. It incorporates a number of noneconomic motives by stressing the impact social context has in real life. Identity as the individual's self-image gets to the center of individual choices. If monetary factors are constant, any choices in conflict with identity are avoided. The conclusions of previous economic analyses may change substantially.

While standard consumption bundles are allocated by "garden-variety tastes," identity and norms are based on social context. The core of the new theory relies on an identity formation relationship in the spirit of Gary Becker's home production function relating the identity of an actor to all his

K. F. Zimmermann (✉)
Global Labor Organization (GLO), UNU-MERIT and Maastricht University, Essen, Germany

© Springer Nature Switzerland AG 2019
B. S. Frey, C. A. Schaltegger (eds.), *21st Century Economics*,
https://doi.org/10.1007/978-3-030-17740-9_61

or her own and all others' actions and the difference between individual characteristics and the norms in the assigned social categories. It now matters for identity and the utility derived from the self-image in what way individuals act contrary to or in line with the norms of the social groups they belong to. A new type of externality may also arise when individuals' utility is affected by the departure of other actors from those social norms. It is important to note that tastes remain independent of social context and individual preferences are given. Social context drives identity formation, but individual identity is captured fully by the entire augmented utility function.

George A. Akerlof and Rachel E. Kranton have developed the concept in a series of articles since 2000 and have outlined their insights in a well-known book written for a wider audience (2010). The importance of identity was also observed in disciplines like anthropology, psychology, sociology, philosophy, or subfields of economics like culture, gender, or ethnicity. Issues of measurement, determinants, and the effects on economic behavior are also frequently investigated. *Identity Economics* is a theoretical analysis that encompasses the idea into traditional economic analysis and outlines its potential for a variety of real-life challenges like organizations, education, gender, race, and poverty. The book illustrates that economics can be realistic and fun.

The authors "know that there is little distance between assumption and result (p. 118)" in their approach. Its value lies in the new assumptions that enable a significantly different view of reality: loyal workers need lower incentive payments in organizations like trade unions, the military, and churches. Generated by societal norms, individuals labeled male or female work in different occupations, and female wages will be lower, even with similar education. "Many African Americans seem to choose courses of action that middle-class white and black Americans consider disastrous," although their rate of return to schooling is higher than for whites. In all cases, individuals seem to trade off lower wages against higher social status. More empirical studies will provide possibilities to evaluate relevance and relative weight of identity and shed more light on identity formation and the evolution of norms.

Literature

Akerlof, G. A., & Kranton, R. E. (2010). *Identity economics. How our identities shape our work, wages, and well-being.* Princeton, NJ: Princeton University Press.

Postscript

Bruno S. Frey and Christoph A. Schaltegger

Contributors to This Book

The present book on *21st Century Economics: Economic Ideas You Should Read and Remember* contains 61 recommendations by the same number of scholars: 26 contributions are from Switzerland, 15 from Germany, 6 from the United States, 2 from the United Kingdom, 4 from Austria, 3 each from Italy and the Netherlands, and the remainder from other countries.

The recommendations given of what the individual scholars judge to be important for present-day economics vary widely. Most recommendations are to articles published in academic journals (62%); the others refer to books or government publications. All the contributors suggest the readers consult texts in English, though it would have been admissible to recommend a contribution written in another language. This reflects the dominance of the English language in present-day economics. There is also a clear dominance of

B. S. Frey (✉)
CREMA – Center for Research in Economics, Management and the Arts, Zurich, Switzerland

CREW – Center for Research in Economics and Well-Being, University of Basel, Basel, Switzerland
e-mail: bruno.frey@bsfrey.ch

C. A. Schaltegger
University of Lucerne, Lucerne, Switzerland
e-mail: Christoph.Schaltegger@unilu.ch

© Springer Nature Switzerland AG 2019
B. S. Frey, C. A. Schaltegger (eds.), *21st Century Economics*,
https://doi.org/10.1007/978-3-030-17740-9_62

economics as practiced in the United States. Of the 61 contributions, no less than 47 (77%) recommend a text originating in the United States. While this has been a much-noted feature of postwar economics, it is interesting to note that the contributors from the many different countries consider the American dominance in economics to exist in the twenty-first century too.

Topics Recommended

The contributions in this volume cover a wide range of issues. This does not come as a surprise since the editors gave no hints with regard to content. Most authors have chosen literature circling around fundamental questions in economic thinking and methodological aspects in economics. Many reviews recommend political economy contributions explaining the impact of specific democratic arrangements and government behavior and tackling specific public policy challenges ranging from public finances over income distribution and social mobility to crime, trade, and finance. A number of papers point to important findings in behavioral economics as well as to educational, labor market and gender aspects. Some authors recommend readings with a focus on inequality aspects in our society, while others recommend papers concerned with environmental questions. Many proposed readings are empirical in their methods, while few point to papers with a focus on formal economic theory. One issue, namely, identity economics, attracted the attention of four authors; this is taken to be a particularly important topic for the future.

It is interesting to note that our selection of authors recommends readings mostly concerned with societal questions and often going beyond a narrow definition of the science of economics. The volume is thus also a nice collection of reviews to show how inspiring economics of the twenty-first century can be and how important the tools of economic thinking are in order to understand real-world challenges and to shape decisions in a society.

Participation Rate

The editors invited 202 academic scholars to participate, of whom 61 (30%) sent in their recommendations. There are considerable differences according to the countries in which the authors presently live. While 50% of the scholars from Germany, and 54% from Switzerland, accepted the invitation, the share for the United States is only 8%. The participation share is also relatively low in the United Kingdom (13%), but it is considerably larger than in the United States.

Several reasons for this marked difference come to mind.

In contrast to European economists, Anglo-Saxon economists:

- may have lower benefits from contributing their thoughts to a collection of short articles than economists from Germany, Austria, and Switzerland, who are under less pressure to publish in scientific journals and therefore can afford the time to engage in an endeavor such as ours.
- may have higher cost of recommending a text written by another economist in the United States or United Kingdom. They may feel that they hurt colleagues to whom they are personally connected and who expect that one of their texts should have been recommended. This cost is lower for a European economist because only few believe that many European economists have made a really important contribution to economics in the twenty-first century. Naming texts by American economists leads to less friction with colleagues in the same department or university.
- may be under more time pressure than European academics, at least in the period between receiving the invitation and the time to hand in the manuscript.

The high participation rate of continental European economists is remarkable, as they have to write their text in a foreign language. It shows that presently European economists are well versed in that language so that they experience little additional effort to write a text in English.

Comparison Between Economic Ideas to Remember and Economic Ideas to Forget

In 2017, Frey, one of the editors of this volume, published with David Iselin a book entitled, *Economic Ideas You Should Forget* in the same format: each contribution must be short (3500 characters); it must relate to one idea; and it must be written by a single author in order to clearly establish responsibility. In the present book, the invitees had to recommend a text written since the year 2000 by a particular author (or several ones), while in the earlier book on *Forgetting*, a general idea could be presented without necessarily naming authors.

Participation rate:

- *Economic Ideas You Should Forget*: Invited persons 179; delivered contributions 71 (i.e., 40%)
- *Economic Ideas You Should Read and Remember*: Invited persons 202; delivered contributions 61 (i.e., 30%)

The lower participation rate in the present book may be due to various reasons:

- As the same approach is repeated (albeit with different second editors), it may be less attractive to participate. This explanation is not very convincing because the first book on *Economic Ideas You Should Forget* was favorably reviewed in a prominent place (Colander 2017; it is the first of the books reviewed in the *Journal of Economic Literature* of September 2017).
- The time pressure for invited scholars may have been more severe in the case of the present book. Indeed, many persons declining the invitation wrote us that they would have enjoyed contributing to the new book but that they could not find the time to do so. However, the scarcity of time is a recurrent phenomenon, and it is not clear why it holds more for the second than for the first book. Almost all the invitees are active as professors. They continually recommend texts to read and remember to their students.
- Perhaps the most important reason for the lower participation rate is that it is more difficult to build up and to be positive than to dismiss and to be negative. This tendency is well known from the classical and social media, which have a strong preference for reporting about negative events rather than positive ones. Economists do not seem to be much different, which is in line with the charge of economics being a "dismal science." This derogative identification of the science of economics has many different meanings (see, e.g., recently Tirole 2017; Rodrik 2017), but it may be understood to mean that economists are quite eager to destroy ideas they take to be outlived but are more reluctant to identify worthy new ideas. This interpretation is supported by several articles in *The Economist* (e.g., Roper 2017), as well as by the well-known dissident Marglin (2012).

An (Informal) Quasi-Experiment

This book can be considered an informal experiment in the sense that the same format has been used to induce potential authors to evaluate ideas in economics; in the first book, it was dismissing bad ideas and in the second identifying good ideas. This certainly is not a tightly controlled approach. Obviously, several conditions have changed between the first and second collections of views. Nevertheless, the two collections are similar enough to make some interesting comparisons. This is in particular the case because most of the scholars who contributed to the *Forget* book have been asked to also participate in the *Read and Remember* book (seven scholars were not asked again for various reasons; two of them died in the meantime).

American economists are generally acknowledged to be forward looking and to have a positive attitude toward new developments. This is well described by the Nobel Prize winner Alvin Roth (2018, p. 1609), who states "… economists are generally enthusiastic about finding new ways to explore the large swath of human behavior that make up economics."

The two editors were therefore convinced that the share of American economists in the collection asking to promote positive economic ideas would be much higher than in the collection asking to discard economic ideas. In contrast, European economists are often taken to be backward looking and afraid of committing themselves to new ideas.

To our great surprise, our quasi-experiment showed the opposite result. While in the book asking to discard economic ideas, 15% of the American invitees participated, in the book asking to identify positive new economic ideas, only 8% participated. The same reduction can be observed for British economists: 58% participated in the first book but only 13% in the second. In contrast, the participation rates of German and Swiss economists remained high, (they only fell from 63% to 50% and 67% to 54%, respectively), and for Austrians it remained the same (100% for both books). The German-speaking economists nowadays seem to be more outspoken and forward looking than usually thought.

The high participation rate of these economists may be attributed to several reasons:

- The editors have more personal contacts to German-speaking economists. The invitees may even feel a sort of obligation toward the editors to participate. This certainly explains the higher absolute participation rate by German-speaking economists but not the fact that the American participation rate more than halved (from 15% to 8%), while the reduction in the participation rate by German-speaking economists is much smaller.
- The pressure to publish in top-ranked scientific journals is stronger for American scholars than German-speaking ones. This may be true but does not explain the much stronger reduction in the participation rate by American economists. If that pressure was so strong, the latter should also have contributed less to the first book.

* European economists may have lower costs in specifically recommending a particular contribution than have Americans, who work in a more closely knit academic environment. As continental European economists mostly recommend reading and remembering contributions by Anglo-Saxon economists, they are less likely to get into trouble with their colleagues. In relative terms, this lowers the strain of pointing out a specific contribution compared to more generally discarding economic ideas without having to give particular names of authors.

The editors believe that this collection of recommendations of what economic ideas to read and to remember produced in the twenty-first century is useful for accomplished academics but in particular also for younger persons engaging in a scientific career in economics. It indicates the views of a large and diverse set of scholars in what directions future research is likely to go.

Literature

Colander, D. (2017). Review of Frey and Iselin, economic ideas you should forget. *Journal of Economic Literature, 55*(3), 1136–1138.

Frey, B. S., & Iselin, D. (2017). *Economic ideas you should forget*. Cham: Springer.

Marglin, S. (2012). Economics: the dismal science? In J. F. Gerber et al. (Eds.), *Towards an integrated paradigm of heterodox economics* (pp. 164–175). London: Palgrave Macmillan.

Rodrik, D. (2017). *Economics rules. The rights and wrongs of the dismal science*. Oxford: Oxford University Press.

Roper, A. (2017, April 11). The dismal science remains dismal, say scientists. *The Economist*.

Roth, A. E. (2018). Marketplaces, markets and market design. *American Economic Review, 108*(7), 1609–1658.

Tirole, J. (2017). *Economics of the common good*. Princeton, NJ: Princeton University Press.

CPSIA information can be obtained
at www.ICGtesting.com
Printed in the USA
LVHW041607280719
625632LV00005B/149/P

9 783030 177393